THE STORY
OF A MINE

BRET HARTE

1st WORLD
LIBRARY
Literary Society

The Story of a Mine

Bret Harte

© 1st World Library, 2007
PO Box 2211
Fairfield, IA 52556
www.1stworldlibrary.com
First Edition

LCCN: 2007934089

Softcover ISBN: 978-1-4218-9627-4
Hardcover ISBN: 978-1-4218-9727-1
eBook ISBN: 978-1-4218-9527-7

Purchase *"The Story of a Mine"*
as a traditional bound book at:
www.1stWorldLibrary.com/purchase.asp?ISBN=978-1-4218-9627-4

1st World Library is a literary, educational organization
dedicated to:

- Creating a free internet library of downloadable ebooks

- Hosting writing competitions and offering book publishing
scholarships.

Interested in more 1st World Library books? contact:
literacy@1stworldlibrary.com
Check us out at: www.1stworldlibrary.com

1st World Library Literary Society

Giving Back to the World

"If you want to work on the core problem, it's early school literacy."

- James Barksdale, former CEO of Netscape

"No skill is more crucial to the future of a child, or to a democratic and prosperous society, than literacy."

- Los Angeles Times

"Literacy... means far more than learning how to read and write... The aim is to transmit... knowledge and promote social participation."

- UNESCO

"Literacy is not a luxury, it is a right and a responsibility. If our world is to meet the challenges of the twenty-first century we must harness the energy and creativity of all our citizens."

- President Bill Clinton

"Parents should be encouraged to read to their children, and teachers should be equipped with all available techniques for teaching literacy, so the varying needs and capacities of individual kids can be taken into account."

- Hugh Mackay

UDO BRACHVOGEL, Esq.,

Whose clever translations of my writings have helped to introduce me to the favor of his countrymen, both here and in Germany, this little volume is heartily dedicated.

BRET HARTE.

New York, December, 1877.

PART—I

CHAPTER I

WHO SOUGHT IT

It was a steep trail leading over the Monterey Coast Range. Concho was very tired, Concho was very dusty, Concho was very much disgusted. To Concho's mind there was but one relief for these insurmountable difficulties, and that lay in a leathern bottle slung over the machillas of his saddle. Concho raised the bottle to his lips, took a long draught, made a wry face, and ejaculated:

"Carajo!"

It appeared that the bottle did not contain aguardiente, but had lately been filled in a tavern near Tres Pinos by an Irishman who sold had American whisky under that pleasing Castilian title. Nevertheless Concho had already nearly emptied the bottle, and it fell back against the saddle as yellow and flaccid as his own cheeks. Thus reinforced Concho turned to look at the valley behind him, from which he had climbed since noon. It was a sterile waste bordered here and there by arable fringes and valdas of meadow land, but in the main, dusty, dry, and forbidding. His eye rested for a moment on a low white cloud line on the eastern horizon, but so mocking and unsubstantial that it seemed to come and go as he gazed. Concho struck his forehead and winked his hot eyelids. Was it the Sierras or the cursed American whisky?

Again he recommenced the ascent. At times the half-worn, half-visible trail became utterly lost in the bare black outcrop of the ridge, but his sagacious mule soon found it again, until, stepping upon a loose boulder, she slipped and fell. In vain Concho tried to lift her from out the ruin of camp kettles, prospecting pans, and picks; she remained quietly recumbent, occasionally raising her head as if to contemplatively glance over the arid plain below. Then he had recourse to useless blows. Then he essayed profanity of a secular kind, such as "Assassin," "Thief," "Beast with a pig's head," "Food for the Bull's Horns," but with no effect.

Then he had recourse to the curse ecclesiastic:

"Ah, Judas Iscariot! is it thus, renegade and traitor, thou leavest me, thy master, a league from camp and supper waiting? Stealer of the Sacrament, get up!"

Still no effect. Concho began to feel uneasy; never before had a mule of pious lineage failed to respond to this kind of exhortation. He made one more desperate attempt:

"Ah, defiler of the altar! lie not there! Look!" he threw his hand into the air, extending the fingers suddenly. "Behold, fiend! I exorcise thee! Ha! tremblest! Look but a little now,—see! Apostate! I—I—excommunicate thee,—Mula!"

"What are you kicking up such a devil of row down there for?" said a gruff voice from the rocks above.

Concho shuddered. Could it be that the devil was really

going to fly away with his mule? He dared not look up.

"Come now," continued the voice, "you just let up on that mule, you d—d old Greaser. Don't you see she's slipped her shoulder?"

Alarmed as Concho was at the information, he could not help feeling to a certain extent relieved. She was lamed, but had not lost her standing as a good Catholic.

He ventured to lift his eyes. A stranger—an Americano from his dress and accent—was descending the rocks toward him. He was a slight-built man with a dark, smooth face, that would have been quite commonplace and inexpressive but for his left eye, in which all that was villainous in him apparently centered. Shut that eye, and you had the features and expression of an ordinary man; cover up those features, and the eye shone out like Eblis's own. Nature had apparently observed this too, and had, by a paralysis of the nerve, ironically dropped the corner of the upper lid over it like a curtain, laughed at her handiwork, and turned him loose to prey upon a credulous world.

"What are you doing here?" said the stranger after he had assisted Concho in bringing the mule to her feet, and a helpless halt.

"Prospecting, Senor."

The stranger turned his respectable right eye toward Concho, while his left looked unutterable scorn and wickedness over the landscape.

"Prospecting, what for?"

"Gold and silver, Senor,—yet for silver most."

"Alone?"

"Of us there are four."

The stranger looked around.

"In camp,—a league beyond," explained the Mexican.

"Found anything?"

"Of this—much." Concho took from his saddle bags a lump of greyish iron ore, studded here and there with star points of pyrites. The stranger said nothing, but his eye looked a diabolical suggestion.

"You are lucky, friend Greaser."

"Eh?"

"It IS silver."

"How know you this?"

"It is my business. I'm a metallurgist."

"And you can say what shall be silver and what is not."

"Yes,—see here!" The stranger took from his saddle bags a little leather case containing some half dozen phials. One, enwrapped in dark-blue paper, he held up to Concho.

"This contains a preparation of silver."

Concho's eyes sparkled, but he looked doubtingly at the stranger.

"Get me some water in your pan."

Concho emptied his water bottle in his prospecting pan and handed it to the stranger. He dipped a dried blade of grass in the bottle and then let a drop fall from its tip in the water. The water remained unchanged.

"Now throw a little salt in the water," said the stranger.

Concho did so. Instantly a white film appeared on the surface, and presently the whole mass assumed a milky hue.

Concho crossed himself hastily, "Mother of God, it is magic!"

"It is chloride of silver, you darned fool."

Not content with this cheap experiment, the stranger then took Concho's breath away by reddening some litmus paper with the nitrate, and then completely knocked over the simple Mexican by restoring its color by dipping it in the salt water.

"You shall try me this," said Concho, offering his iron ore to the stranger;—"you shall use the silver and the salt."

"Not so fast my friend," answered the stranger; "in the first place this ore must be melted, and then a chip taken and put in shape like this,—and that is worth something, my Greaser cherub. No, sir, a man don't spend all his youth at Freiburg and Heidelburg to throw away his science gratuitously on the first Greaser he meets."

"It will cost—eh—how much?" said the Mexican eagerly.

"Well, I should say it would take about a hundred dollars and expenses to—to—find silver in that ore. But once you've got it there—you're all right for tons of it."

"You shall have it," said the now excited Mexican. "You shall have it of us,—the four! You shall come to our camp and shall melt it,—and show the silver, and—enough! Come!" and in his feverishness he clutched the hand of his companion as if to lead him forth at once.

"What are you going to do with your mule?" said the stranger.

"True, Holy Mother,—what, indeed?"

"Look yer," said the stranger, with a grim smile, "she won't stray far, I'll be bound. I've an extra pack mule above here; you can ride on her, and lead me into camp, and to-morrow come back for your beast."

Poor honest Concho's heart sickened at the prospect of leaving behind the tired servant he had objurgated so strongly a moment before, but the love of gold was uppermost. "I will come back to thee, little one, to-morrow, a rich man. Meanwhile, wait thou here, patient one,—Adios!— thou smallest of mules,—Adios!"

And, seizing the stranger's hand, he clambered up the rocky ledge until they reached the summit. Then the stranger turned and gave one sweep of his malevolent eye over the valley.

Wherefore, in after years, when their story was related, with the devotion of true Catholic pioneers, they named the mountain "La Canada de la Visitacion del Diablo," "The Gulch of the Visitation of the Devil," the same being now the boundary lines of one of the famous Mexican land grants.

CHAPTER II

WHO FOUND IT

Concho was so impatient to reach the camp and deliver his good news to his companions that more than once the stranger was obliged to command him to slacken his pace. "Is it not enough, you infernal Greaser, that you lame your own mule, but you must try your hand on mine? Or am I to put Jinny down among the expenses?" he added with a grin and a slight lifting of his baleful eyelid.

When they had ridden a mile along the ridge, they began to descend again toward the valley. Vegetation now sparingly bordered the trail, clumps of chemisal, an occasional manzanita bush, and one or two dwarfed "buckeyes" rooted their way between the interstices of the black-gray rock. Now and then, in crossing some dry gully, worn by the overflow of winter torrents from above, the grayish rock gloom was relieved by dull red and brown masses of color, and almost every overhanging rock bore the mark of a miner's pick. Presently, as they rounded the curving flank of the mountain, from a rocky bench below them, a thin ghost-like stream of smoke seemed to be steadily drawn by invisible hands into the invisible ether. "It is the camp," said Concho, gleefully; "I will myself forward to prepare them for the stranger," and before his companion could detain him, he had disappeared at a sharp canter around the curve of the trail.

Left to himself, the stranger took a more leisurely pace, which left him ample time for reflection. Scamp as he was, there was something in the simple credulity of poor Concho that made him uneasy. Not that his moral consciousness was touched, but he feared that Concho's companions might, knowing Concho's simplicity, instantly suspect him of trading upon it. He rode on in a deep study. Was he reviewing his past life? A vagabond by birth and education, a swindler by profession, an outcast by reputation, without absolutely turning his back upon respectability, he had trembled on the perilous edge of criminality ever since his boyhood. He did not scruple to cheat these Mexicans,—they were a degraded race,—and for a moment he felt almost an accredited agent of progress and civilization. We never really understand the meaning of enlightenment until we begin to use it aggressively.

A few paces further on four figures appeared in the now gathering darkness of the trail. The stranger quickly recognized the beaming smile of Concho, foremost of the party. A quick glance at the faces of the others satisfied him that while they lacked Concho's good humor, they certainly did not surpass him in intellect. "Pedro" was a stout vaquero. "Manuel" was a slim half-breed and ex-convert of the Mission of San Carmel, and "Miguel" a recent butcher of Monterey. Under the benign influences of Concho that suspicion with which the ignorant regard strangers died away, and the whole party escorted the stranger—who had given his name as Mr. Joseph Wiles—to their camp-fire. So anxious were they to begin their experiments that even the instincts of hospitality were forgotten, and it was not until Mr. Wiles—now known as "Don Jose"—sharply reminded them that he wanted some "grub," that they came to their senses. When the frugal meal of tortillas, frijoles, salt pork, and chocolate was over, an oven was built of the dark-red rock brought from the ledge before them, and an earthenware jar, glazed by some peculiar local process, tightly fitted over it, and packed with clay and sods. A fire was speedily built of pine boughs continually brought from a wooded ravine below, and in a few moments the furnace was in full blast. Mr. Wiles did not participate in these active preparations, except to give occasional directions between his teeth, which were contemplatively fixed over a clay pipe as he lay comfortably on his back on the ground. Whatever enjoyment the rascal may have had in their useless labors he did not show it, but it was observed that his left eye often followed the broad figure of the ex-vaquero, Pedro, and often dwelt on that worthy's beetling brows and half-savage face. Meeting that baleful glance once, Pedro growled out an oath, but could not resist a hideous fascination that caused him again and again to seek it.

The scene was weird enough without Wiles's eye to add to its wild picturesqueness. The mountain towered above,—a heavy Rembrandtish mass of black shadow,—sharply cut here and there against a sky so inconceivably remote that the world-sick soul must have despaired of ever reaching so far, or of climbing its steel-blue walls. The stars were large, keen, and brilliant, but cold and steadfast. They did not dance nor twinkle in their adamantine setting. The furnace fire painted the faces of the men an Indian red, glanced on brightly colored blanket and serape, but was eventually caught and absorbed in the waiting shadows of the black mountain, scarcely twenty feet from the furnace door. The low, half-sung, half-whispered foreign speech of the group, the roaring of the furnace, and the quick, sharp yelp of a coyote on the plain below were the only sounds that broke the awful silence of the hills.

It was almost dawn when it was announced that the ore had fused. And it was high time, for the pot was slowly sinking into the fast-crumbling oven. Concho uttered a jubilant "God and Liberty," but Don Jose Wiles bade him be silent and bring stakes to support the pot. Then Don Jose bent over the seething mass. It was for a moment only. But in that moment this accomplished metallurgist, Mr. Joseph Wiles, had quietly dropped a silver half dollar into the pot!

Then he charged them to keep up the fires and went to sleep—all but one eye.

Dawn came with dull beacon fires on the near hill tops, and, far in the East, roses over the Sierran snow. Birds twittering in the alder fringes a mile below, and the creaking of wagon wheels,—the wagon itself a mere cloud of dust in the distant road,—were heard distinctly. Then the melting pot was solemnly broken by Don Jose, and the glowing incandescent mass turned into the road to cool.

And then the metallurgist chipped a small fragment from the mass and pounded it, and chipped another smaller piece and pounded that, and then subjected it to acid, and then treated it to a salt bath which became at once milky,—and at last produced a white something,—mirabile dictu!—two cents' worth of silver!

Concho shouted with joy; the rest gazed at each other doubtingly and distrustfully; companions in poverty, they began to diverge and suspect each other in prosperity. Wiles's left eye glanced ironically from the one to the other.

"Here is the hundred dollars, Don Jose," said Pedro, handing the gold to Wiles with a decidedly brusque intimation that the services and presence of a stranger were no longer required.

Wiles took the money with a gracious smile and a wink that sent Pedro's heart into his boots, and was turning away, when a cry from Manuel stopped him. "The pot,—the pot,—it has leaked! look! behold! see!"

He had been cleaning away the crumbled fragments of the furnace to get ready for breakfast, and had disclosed a shining pool of QUICKSILVER!

Wiles started, cast a rapid glance around the group, saw in a flash that the metal was unknown to them,—and then said quietly:

"It is not silver."

"Pardon, Senor, it is, and still molten." Wiles stooped and ran his fingers through the shining metal.

"Mother of God,—what is it then?—magic?"

"No, only base metal." But here, Concho, emboldened by Wiles's experiment, attempted to seize a handful of the glistening mass, that instantly broke through his fingers in a thousand tiny spherules, and even sent a few globules up his shirt sleeves, until he danced around in mingled fear and childish pleasure.

"And it is not worth the taking?" queried Pedro of Wiles.

Wiles's right eye and bland face were turned toward the speaker, but his malevolent left was glancing at the dull red-brown rock on the hill side.

"No!"—and turning abruptly away, he proceeded to saddle his mule.

Manuel, Miguel, and Pedro, left to themselves, began talking earnestly together, while Concho, now mindful of his crippled mule, made his way back to the trail where he had left her. But she was no longer there. Constant to her master through beatings and bullyings, she could not stand incivility and inattention. There are certain qualities of the sex that belong to all animated nature.

Inconsolable, footsore, and remorseful, Concho returned to the camp and furnace, three miles across the rocky ridge. But what was his astonishment on arriving to find the place deserted of man, mule, and camp equipage. Concho called aloud. Only the echoing rocks grimly answered him. Was it a trick? Concho tried to laugh. Ah—yes—a good one,—a joke,—no—no—they HAD deserted him. And then poor Concho bowed his head to the ground, and falling on his face, cried as if his honest heart would break.

The tempest passed in a moment; it was not Concho's nature to suffer long nor brood over an injury. As he raised his head again his eye caught the shimmer of the quicksilver,—that pool of merry antic metal that had so delighted him an hour before. In a few moments Concho was again disporting with it; chasing it here and there, rolling it in his palms and laughing with boy-like glee at its elusive freaks and fancies. "Ah, sprightly one,—skipjack,—there thou goest,—come here. This way,—now I have thee, little one,—come, much-acha,—come and kiss me," until he had quite forgotten the defection of his companions. And even when he shouldered his sorry pack, he was fain to carry his playmate away with him in his empty leathern flask.

And yet I fancy the sun looked kindly on him as he strode cheerily down the black mountain side, and his step was none the less free nor light that he carried with him neither the brilliant prospects nor the crime of his late comrades.

CHAPTER III

WHO CLAIMED IT

The fog had already closed in on Monterey, and was now rolling, a white, billowy sea above, that soon shut out the blue breakers below. Once or twice in descending the mountain Concho had overhung the cliff and looked down upon the curving horse-shoe of a bay below him,—distant yet many miles. Earlier in the afternoon he had seen the gilt cross on the white-faced Mission flare in the sunlight, but now all was gone. By the time he reached the highway of the town it was quite dark, and he plunged into the first fonda at the wayside, and endeavored to forget his woes and his weariness in aguardiente. But Concho's head ached, and his back ached, and he was so generally distressed that he bethought him of a medico,—an American doctor,—lately come into the town, who had once treated Concho and his mule with apparently the same medicine, and after the same heroic fashion. Concho reasoned, not illogically, that if he were to be physicked at all he ought to get the worth of his money. The grotesque extravagance of life, of fruit and vegetables, in California was inconsistent with infinitesimal doses. In Concho's previous illness the doctor had given him a dozen 4 grain quinine powders.

The following day the grateful Mexican walked into the

Doctor's office—cured. The Doctor was gratified until, on examination, it appeared that to save trouble, and because his memory was poor, Concho had taken all the powders in one dose. The Doctor shrugged his shoulders and—altered his practice.

"Well," said Dr. Guild, as Concho sank down exhaustedly in one of the Doctor's two chairs, "what now? Have you been sleeping again in the tule marshes, or are you upset with commissary whisky? Come, have it out."

But Concho declared that the devil was in his stomach, that Judas Iscariot had possessed himself of his spine, that imps were in his forehead, and that his feet had been scourged by Pontius Pilate.

"That means 'blue mass,'" said the Doctor. And gave it to him,—a bolus as large as a musket ball, and as heavy.

Concho took it on the spot, and turned to go.

"I have no money, Senor Medico."

"Never mind. It's only a dollar, the price of the medicine."

Concho looked guilty at having gulped down so much cash. Then he said timidly:

"I have no money, but I have got here what is fine and jolly. It is yours." And he handed over the contents of the precious tin can he had brought with him.

The Doctor took it, looked at the shivering volatile mass and said, "Why this is quicksilver!"

Concho laughed, "Yes, very quick silver, so!" and he

snapped his fingers to show its sprightliness.

The Doctor's face grew earnest; "Where did you get this, Concho?" he finally asked.

"It ran from the pot in the mountains beyond."

The Doctor looked incredulous. Then Concho related the whole story.

"Could you find that spot again?"

"Madre de Dios, yes,—I have a mule there; may the devil fly away with her!"

"And you say your comrades saw this?"

"Why not?"

"And you say they afterwards left you,—deserted you?"

"They did, ingrates!"

The Doctor arose and shut his office door. "Hark ye, Concho," he said, "that bit of medicine I gave you just now was worth a dollar, it was worth a dollar because the material of which it was composed was made from the stuff you have in that can,—quicksilver or mercury. It is one of the most valuable of metals, especially in a gold-mining country. My good fellow, if you know where to find enough of it, your fortune is made."

Concho rose to his feet.

"Tell me, was the rock you built your furnace of red?"

"Si, Senor."

"And brown?"

"Si, Senor."

"And crumbled under the heat?"

"As to nothing."

"And did you see much of this red rock?"

"The mountain mother is in travail with it."

"Are you sure that your comrades have not taken possession of the mountain mother?"

"As how?"

"By claiming its discovery under the mining laws, or by pre-emption?"

"They shall not."

"But how will you, single-handed, fight the four; for I doubt not your scientific friend has a hand in it?"

"I will fight."

"Yes, my Concho, but suppose I take the fight off your hands. Now, here's a proposition: I will get half a dozen Americanos to go in with you. You will have to get money to work the mine,—you will need funds. You shall share half with them. They will take the risk, raise the money, and protect you."

Bret Harte

"I see," said Concho, nodding his head and winking his eyes rapidly. "Bueno!"

"I will return in ten minutes," said the Doctor, taking his hat.

He was as good as his word. In ten minutes he returned with six original locaters, a board of directors, a president, secretary, and a deed of incorporation of the 'Blue Mass Quicksilver Mining Co.' This latter was a delicate compliment to the Doctor, who was popular. The President added to these necessary articles a revolver.

"Take it," he said, handing over the weapon to Concho. "Take it; my horse is outside; take that, ride like h—l and hang on to the claim until we come!"

In another moment Concho was in the saddle. Then the mining director lapsed into the physician.

"I hardly know," said Dr. Guild, doubtfully, "if in your present condition you ought to travel. You have just taken a powerful medicine," and the Doctor looked hypocritically concerned.

"Ah,—the devil!" laughed Concho, "what is the quicksilver that is IN to that which is OUT? Hoopa, la Mula!" and, with a clatter of hoofs and jingle of spurs, was presently lost in the darkness.

"You were none too soon, gentlemen," said the American Alcalde, as he drew up before the Doctor's door. "Another company has just been incorporated for the same location, I reckon."

"Who are they?"

"Three Mexicans,—Pedro, Manuel, and Miguel, headed by that d—d cock-eyed Sydney Duck, Wiles."

"Are they here?"

"Manuel and Miguel, only. The others are over at Tres Pinos lally-gaging Roscommon and trying to rope him in to pay off their whisky bills at his grocery."

"If that's so we needn't start before sunrise, for they're sure to get roaring drunk."

And this legitimate successor of the grave Mexican Alcaldes, having thus delivered his impartial opinion, rode away.

Meanwhile, Concho the redoubtable, Concho the fortunate, spared neither riata nor spur. The way was dark, the trail obscure and at times even dangerous, and Concho, familiar as he was with these mountain fastnesses, often regretted his sure-footed Francisquita. "Care not, O Concho," he would say to himself, "'tis but a little while, only a little while, and thou shalt have another Francisquita to bless thee. Eh, skipjack, there was a fine music to thy dancing. A dollar for an ounce,—'tis as good as silver, and merrier." Yet for all his good spirits he kept a sharp lookout at certain bends of the mountain trail; not for assassins or brigands, for Concho was physically courageous, but for the Evil One, who, in various forms, was said to lurk in the Santa Cruz Range, to the great discomfort of all true Catholics. He recalled the incident of Ignacio, a muleteer of the Franciscan Friars, who, stopping at the Angelus to repeat the Credo, saw Luzbel plainly in the likeness of a monstrous grizzly bear, mocking him by sitting on his haunches and lifting his paws, clasped together, as if in prayer. Nevertheless, with one hand grasping his reins and his rosary, and the other clutching his whisky flask and revolver, he fared on so rapidly that he reached the summit

Bret Harte

as the earlier streaks of dawn were outlining the far-off Sierran peaks. Tethering his horse on a strip of tableland, he descended cautiously afoot until he reached the bench, the wall of red rock and the crumbled and dismantled furnace. It was as he had left it that morning; there was no trace of recent human visitation. Revolver in hand, Concho examined every cave, gully, and recess, peered behind trees, penetrated copses of buckeye and manzanita, and listened. There was no sound but the faint soughing of the wind over the pines below him. For a while he paced backward and forward with a vague sense of being a sentinel, but his mercurial nature soon rebelled against this monotony, and soon the fatigues of the day began to tell upon him. Recourse to his whisky flask only made him the drowsier, until at last he was fain to lie down and roll himself up tightly in his blanket. The next moment he was sound asleep.

His horse neighed twice from the summit, but Concho heard him not. Then the brush crackled on the ledge above him, a small fragment of rock rolled near his feet, but he stirred not. And then two black figures were outlined on the crags beyond.

"St-t-t!" whispered a voice. "There is one lying beside the furnace." The speech was Spanish, but the voice was Wiles's.

The other figure crept cautiously to the edge of the crag and looked over. "It is Concho, the imbecile," said Pedro, contemptuously.

"But if he should not be alone, or if he should waken?"

"I will watch and wait. Go you and affix the notification."

Wiles disappeared. Pedro began to creep down the face of

the rocky ledge, supporting himself by chemisal and brush-wood.

The next moment Pedro stood beside the unconscious man. Then he looked cautiously around. The figure of his companion was lost in the shadow of the rocks above; only a slight crackle of brush betrayed his whereabouts. Suddenly Pedro flung his serape over the sleeper's head, and then threw his powerful frame and tremendous weight full upon Concho's upturned face, while his strong arms clasped the blanket-pinioned limbs of his victim. There was a momentary upheaval, a spasm, and a struggle; but the tightly-rolled blanket clung to the unfortunate man like cerements.

There was no noise, no outcry, no sound of struggle. There was nothing to be seen but the peaceful, prostrate figures of the two men darkly outlined on the ledge. They might have been sleeping in each other's arms. In the black silence the stealthy tread of Wiles in the brush above was distinctly audible.

Gradually the struggles grew fainter. Then a whisper from the crags:

"I can't see you. What are you doing?"

"Watching!"

"Sleeps he?"

"He sleeps!"

"Soundly?"

"Soundly."

"After the manner of the dead?"

"After the fashion of the dead!"

The last tremor had ceased. Pedro rose as Wiles descended.

"All is ready," said Wiles; "you are a witness of my placing the notifications?"

"I am a witness."

"But of this one?" pointing to Concho. "Shall we leave him here?"

"A drunken imbecile,—why not?"

Wiles turned his left eye on the speaker. They chanced to be standing nearly in the same attitude they had stood the preceding night. Pedro uttered a cry and an imprecation, "Carramba! Take your devil's eye from me! What see you? Eh,—what?"

"Nothing, good Pedro," said Wiles, turning his bland right cheek to Pedro. The infuriated and half-frightened ex-vaquero returned the long knife he had half-drawn from its sheath, and growled surlily: "Go on then! But keep thou on that side, and I will on this." And so, side by side, listening, watching, distrustful of all things, but mainly of each other, they stole back and up into those shadows from which they might like evil spirits have been poetically evoked.

A half hour passed, in which the east brightened, flashed, and again melted into gold. And then the sun came up haughtily, and a fog that had stolen across the summit in the night arose and fled up the mountain side, tearing its white robes in its guilty haste, and leaving them fluttering from tree and crag and scar. A thousand tiny blades, nestling in the crevices of rocks, nurtured in storms and rocked by the trade winds, stretched their wan and feeble arms toward Him; but Concho the strong, Concho the brave, Concho the light-hearted spake not nor stirred.

CHAPTER IV

WHO TOOK IT

There was persistent neighing on the summit. Concho's horse wanted his breakfast.

This protestation reached the ears of a party ascending the mountain from its western face. To one of the party it was familiar.

"Why, blank it all, that's Chiquita. That d—d Mexican's lying drunk somewhere," said the President of the B. M. Co.

"I don't like the look of this at all," said Dr. Guild, as they rode up beside the indignant animal. "If it had been an American, it might have been carelessness, but no Mexican ever forgets his beast. Drive ahead, boys; we may be too late."

In half an hour they came in sight of the ledge below, the crumbled furnace, and the motionless figure of Concho, wrapped in a blanket, lying prone in the sunlight.

"I told you so,—drunk!" said the President.

The Doctor looked grave, but did not speak. They

dismounted and picketed their horses. Then crept on all fours to the ledge above the furnace. There was a cry from Secretary Gibbs, "Look yer. Some fellar has been jumping us, boys. See these notices."

There were two notices on canvas affixed to the rock, claiming the ground, and signed by Pedro, Manuel, Miguel, Wiles, and Roscommon.

"This was done, Doctor, while your trustworthy Greaser locater,—d—n him,—lay there drunk. What's to be done now?"

But the Doctor was making his way to the unfortunate cause of their defeat, lying there quite mute to their reproaches. The others followed him.

The Doctor knelt beside Concho, unrolled him, placed his hand upon his wrist, his ear over his heart, and then said:

"Dead."

"Of course. He got medicine of you last night. This comes of your d—d heroic practice."

But the Doctor was too much occupied to heed the speaker's raillery. He had peered into Concho's protuberant eye, opened his mouth, and gazed at the swollen tongue, and then suddenly rose to his feet.

"Tear down those notices, boys, but keep them. Put up your own. Don't be alarmed, you will not be interfered with, for here is murder added to robbery."

"Murder?"

"Yes," said the Doctor, excitedly, "I'll take my oath on any inquest that this man was strangled to death. He was surprised while asleep. Look here." He pointed to the revolver still in Concho's stiffening hand, which the murdered man had instantly cocked, but could not use in the struggle.

"That's so," said the President, "no man goes to sleep with a cocked revolver. What's to be done?"

"Everything," said the Doctor. "This deed was committed within the last two hours; the body is still warm. The murderer did not come our way, or we should have met him on the trail. He is, if anywhere, between here and Tres Pinos."

"Gentlemen," said the President, with a slight preparatory and half judicial cough, "two of you will stay here and stick! The others will follow me to Tres Pinos. The law has been outraged. You understand the Court!"

By some odd influence the little group of half-cynical, half-trifling, and wholly reckless men had become suddenly sober, earnest citizens. They said, "Go on," nodded their heads, and betook themselves to their horses.

"Had we not better wait for the inquest and swear out a warrant?" said the Secretary, cautiously.

"How many men have we?"

"Five!"

"Then," said the President, summing up the Revised Statutes of the State of California in one strong sentence; "then we don't want no d—d warrant."

CHAPTER V

WHO HAD A LIEN ON IT

It was high noon at Tres Pinos. The three pines from which it gained its name, in the dusty road and hot air, seemed to smoke from their balsamic spires. There was a glare from the road, a glare from the sky, a glare from the rocks, a glare from the white canvas roofs of the few shanties and cabins which made up the village. There was even a glare from the unpainted red-wood boards of Roscommon's grocery and tavern, and a tendency of the warping floor of the veranda to curl up beneath the feet of the intruder. A few mules, near the watering trough, had shrunk within the scant shadow of the corral.

The grocery business of Mr. Roscommon, although adequate and sufficient for the village, was not exhausting nor overtaxing to the proprietor; the refilling of the pork and flour barrel of the average miner was the work of a brief hour on Saturday nights, but the daily replenishment of the average miner with whisky was arduous and incessant. Roscommon spent more time behind his bar than his grocer's counter. Add to this the fact that a long shed-like extension or wing bore the legend, "Cosmopolitan Hotel, Board or Lodging by the Day or Week. M. Roscommon," and you got an idea of the variety of the proprietor's functions. The "hotel," however, was more directly under the charge of Mrs. Roscommon, a lady of thirty years, strong, truculent, and good-hearted.

Mr. Roscommon had early adopted the theory that most of his customers were insane, and were to be alternately bullied or placated, as the case might be. Nothing that occurred, no extravagance of speech nor act, ever ruffled his equilibrium, which was as dogged and stubborn as it was outwardly calm. When not serving liquor, or in the interval while it was being drank, he was always wiping his counter with an exceedingly dirty towel,—or indeed anything that came handy. Miners, noticing this purely perfunctory habit, occasionally supplied him slily with articles inconsistent with their service,— fragments of their shirts and underclothing, flour sacking, tow, and once with a flannel petticoat of his wife's, stolen from the line in the back-yard. Roscommon would continue his wiping without looking up, but yet conscious of the presence of each customer. "And it's not another dhrop ye'll git, Jack Brown, until ye've wiped out the black score that stands agin ye." "And it's there ye are, darlint, and it's here's the bottle that's been lukin' for ye sins Saturday." "And fwhot hev you done with the last I sent ye, ye divil of a McCorkle, and here's me back that's bruk entoirely wid dipping intil the pork barl to giv ye the best sides, and ye spending yur last cint on a tare into Gilroy. Whist! and if it's fer foighting ye are, boys, there's an illigant bit of sod beyant the corral, and it may be meself'll come out with a shtick and be sociable."

On this particular day, however, Mr. Roscommon was not in his usual spirits, and when the clatter of horses' hoofs before the door announced the approach of strangers, he absolutely ceased wiping his counter and looked up as Dr. Guild, the President, and Secretary of the new Company strode into the shop.

"We are looking," said the President, "for a man by the name of Wiles, and three Mexicans known as Pedro, Manuel, and Miguel."

"Ye are?"

"We are!"

"Faix, and I hope ye'll foind 'em. And if ye'll git from 'em the score I've got agin 'em, darlint, I'll add a blessing to it."

There was a laugh at this from the bystanders, who, somehow, resented the intrusion of these strangers.

"I fear you will find it no laughing matter, gentlemen," said Dr. Guild, a little stiffly, "when I tell you that a murder has been committed, and the men I am seeking within an hour of that murder put up that notice signed by their names," and Dr. Guild displayed the paper.

There was a breathless silence among the crowd as they eagerly pressed around the Doctor. Only Roscommon kept on wiping his counter.

"You will observe, gentlemen, that the name of Roscommon also appears on this paper as one of the original beaters."

"And sure, darlint," said Roscommon, without looking up, "if ye've no better ividince agin them boys then you have forninst me, it's home ye'd bether be riding to wanst. For it's meself as hasn't sturred fut out of the store the day and noight,—more betoken as the boys I've sarved kin testify."

"That's so, Ross, right," chorused the crowd, "We've been running the old man all night."

"Then how comes your name on this paper?"

"O murdher! will ye listen to him, boys? As if every felly that owed me a whisky bill didn't come to me and say, 'Ah, Misther Roscommon,' or 'Moike,' as the case moight be, sure it's an illigant sthrike I've made this day, and it's meself that has put down your name as an original locater, and yer fortune's made, Mr. Roscommon, and will yer fill me up another quart for the good luck betune you and me. Ah, but ask Jack Brown over yar if it isn't sick that I am of his original locations."

The laugh that followed this speech, and its practical application, convinced the party that they had blundered, that they could obtain no clue to the real culprits here, and that any attempt by threats would meet violent opposition. Nevertheless the Doctor was persistent:

"When did you see these men last?"

"When did I see them, is it? Bedad, what with sarvin up the liquor and keeping me counters dry and swate, I never see them at all."

"That's so, Ross," chorused the crowd again, to whom the whole proceeding was delightfully farcical.

"Then I can tell you, gentlemen," said the Doctor, stiffly, "that they were in Monterey last night, that they did not return on that trail this morning, and that they must have passed here at daybreak."

With these words, which the Doctor regretted as soon as delivered, the party rode away.

Mr. Roscommon resumed his service and counter wiping.

But late that night, when the bar was closed and the last loiterer was summarily ejected, Mr. Roscommon, in the conjugal privacy of his chamber, produced a legal-looking paper. "Read it, Maggie, darlint, for it's meself never had the larning nor the parts."

Mistress Roscommon took the paper:

"Shure, it's law papers, making over some property to yis. O Moike! ye havn't been spekilating!"

"Whist! and fwhotz that durty gray paper wid the sales and flourishes?"

"Faix, it bothers me intoirely. Shure it oin't in English."

"Whist! Maggie, it's a Spanish grant!"

"A Spanish grant? O Moike, and what did ye giv for it?"

Mr. Roscommon laid his finger beside his nose and said softly, "Whishky!"

PART II—IN THE COURTS

CHAPTER VI

HOW A GRANT WAS GOT FOR IT

While the Blue Mass Company, with more zeal than discretion, were actively pursuing Pedro and Wiles over the road to Tres Pinos, Senors Miguel and Manuel were comfortably seated in a fonda at Monterey, smoking cigarritos and discussing their late discovery. But they were in no better mood than their late companions, and it appeared from their conversation that in an evil moment they had sold out their interest in the alleged silver mine to Wiles and Pedro for a few hundred dollars,—succumbing to what they were assured would be an active opposition on the part of the Americanos. The astute reader will easily understand that the accomplished Mr. Wiles did not inform them of its value as a quicksilver mine, although he was obliged to impart his secret to Pedro as a necessary accomplice and reckless coadjutor. That Pedro felt no qualms of conscience in thus betraying his two comrades may be inferred from his recent direct and sincere treatment of Concho, and that he would, if occasion offered or policy made it expedient, as calmly obliterate Mr. Wiles, that gentleman himself never for a moment doubted.

"If we had waited but a little he would have given more,—this cock-eye!" regretted Manuel querulously.

"Not a peso," said Miguel, firmly.

"And why, my Miguel? Thou knowest we could have worked the mine ourselves."

"Good, and lost even that labor. Look you, little brother. Show to me now the Mexican that has ever made a real of a mine in California. How many, eh? None! Not a one. Who owns the Mexican's mine, eh? Americanos! Who takes the money from the Mexican's mine? Americanos! Thou rememberest Briones, who spent a gold mine to make a silver one? Who has the lands and house of Briones? Americanos! Who has the cattle of Briones? Americanos! Who has the mine of Briones? Americanos! Who has the silver Briones never found? Americanos! Always the same! Forever! Ah! carramba!"

Then the Evil One evidently took it into his head and horns to worry and toss these men—comparatively innocent as they were—still further, for a purpose. For presently to them appeared one Victor Garcia, whilom a clerk of the Ayuntamiento, who rallied them over aguardiente, and told them the story of the quicksilver discovery, and the two mining claims taken out that night by Concho and Wiles. Whereat Manuel exploded with profanity and burnt blue with sulphurous malediction; but Miguel, the recent ecclesiastic, sat livid and thoughtful.

Finally came a pause in Manuel's bombardment, and something like this conversation took place between the cooler actors:

Miguel (thoughtfully). "When was it thou didst petition for

lands in the valley, friend Victor?"

Victor (amazedly). "Never! It is a sterile waste. Am I a fool?"

Miguel (softly). "Thou didst. Of thy Governor, Micheltorena. I have seen the application."

Victor (beginning to appreciate a rodential odor). "Si! I had forgotten. Art thou sure it was in the valley?"

Miguel (persuasively). "In the valley and up the falda."*

> * Falda, or valda, i. e., that part of the skirt of a woman's robe that breaks upon the ground, and is also applied to the final slope of a hill, from the angle that it makes upon the level plain.

Victor (with decision). "Certainly. Of a verity,—the falda likewise."

Miguel (eying Victor). "And yet thou hadst not the grant. Painful is it that it should have been burned with the destruction of the other archives, by the Americanos at Monterey."

Victor (cautiously feeling his way). "Possiblemente."

Miguel. "It might be wise to look into it."

Victor (bluntly). "As why?"

Miguel. "For our good and thine, friend Victor. We bring thee a discovery; thou bringest us thy skill, thy experience, thy government knowledge,—thy Custom House paper."*

* Grants, applications, and official notifications, under the Spanish Government, were drawn on a stamped paper known as custom House paper.

Manuel (breaking in drunkenly). "But for what? We are Mexicans. Are we not fated? We shall lose. Who shall keep the Americanos off?"

Miguel. "We shall take ONE American in! Ha! seest thou? This American comrade shall bribe his courts, his corregidores. After a little he shall supply the men who invent the machine of steam, the mill, the furnace, eh?"

Victor. "But who is he,—not to steal?"

Miguel. "He is that man of Ireland, a good Catholic, at Tres Pinos."

Victor and Manuel (omnes). "Roscommon?"

Miguel. "Of the same. We shall give him a share for the provisions, for the tools, for the aguardiente. It is of the Irish that the Americanos have great fear. It is of them that the votes are made,—that the President is chosen. It is of him that they make the Alcalde in San Francisco. And we are of the Church like him."

They said "Bueno" altogether, and for the moment appeared to be upheld by a religious enthusiasm,—a joint confession of faith that meant death, destruction, and possibly forgery, as against the men who thought otherwise.

This spiritual harmony did away with all practical consideration and doubt. "I have a little niece," said Victor, "whose work with the pen is marvellous. If one says to her, 'Carmen, copy me this, or the other one,'—even if it be copper-plate,—

look you it is done, and you cannot know of which is the original. Madre de Dios! the other day she makes me a rubric* of the Governor, Pio Pico, the same, identical. Thou knowest her, Miguel. She asked concerning thee yesterday."

* The Spanish "rubric" is the complicated flourish attached to a signature, and is as individual and character-istic as the handwriting.

With the embarrassment of an underbred man, Miguel tried to appear unconcerned, but failed dismally. Indeed, I fear that the black eyes of Carmen had already done their perfect and accepted work, and had partly induced the application for Victor's aid. He, however, dissembled so far as to ask:

"But will she not know?"

"She is a child."

"But will she not talk?"

"Not if I say nay, and if thou—eh, Miguel?"

This bit of flattery (which, by the way, was a lie, for Victor's niece did not incline favorably to Miguel), had its effect. They shook hands over the table. "But," said Miguel, "what is to be done must be done now." "At the moment," said Victor, "and thou shalt see it done. Eh? Does it content thee? then come!"

Miguel nodded to Manuel. "We will return in an hour; wait thou here."

They filed out into the dark, irregular street. Fate led them to pass the office of Dr. Guild at the moment that Concho mounted his horse. The shadows concealed them from their rival, but they overheard the last injunctions of the President to the unlucky Concho.

"Thou hearest?" said Miguel, clutching his companion's arm.

"Yes," said Victor. "But let him ride, my friend; in one hour we shall have that that shall arrive YEARS before him," and with a complacent chuckle they passed unseen and unheard until, abruptly turning a corner, they stopped before a low adobe house.

It had once been a somewhat pretentious dwelling, but had evidently followed the fortunes of its late owner, Don Juan Briones, who had offered it as a last sop to the three-headed Cerberus that guarded the El Refugio Plutonean treasures, and who had swallowed it in a single gulp. It was in very bad case. The furrows of its red-tiled roof looked as if they were the results of age and decrepitude. Its best room had a musty smell; there was the dampness of deliquescence in its slow decay, but the Spanish Californians were sensible architects, and its massive walls and partitions defied the earthquake thrill, and all the year round kept an even temperature within.

Victor led Miguel through a low anteroom into a plainly-furnished chamber, where Carmen sat painting.

Now Mistress Carmen was a bit of a painter, in a pretty little way, with all the vague longings of an artist, but without, I fear, the artist's steadfast soul. She recognized beauty and form as a child might, without understanding their meaning, and somehow failed to make them even interpret her woman's moods, which surely were nature's too. So she painted everything with this innocent lust of the eye,—flowers, birds, insects, landscapes, and figures,—with a joyous fidelity, but no particular poetry. The bird never sang to her but one song, the flowers or trees spake but one language, and her skies never brightened except in color. She came out strong on the Catholic saints, and would toss you up a cleanly-shaven Aloysius, sweetly destitute of expression, or a dropsical, lethargic Madonna that you couldn't have told from an old master, so bad it was. Her faculty of faithful reproduction even showed itself in fanciful lettering,—and latterly in the imitation of fabrics and signatures. Indeed, with her eye for beauty of form, she had always excelled in penmanship at the Convent,—an accomplishment which the good sisters held in great repute.

In person she was petite, with a still unformed girlish figure, perhaps a little too flat across the back, and with possibly a too great tendency to a boyish stride in walking. Her brow, covered by blue-black hair, was low and frank and honest; her eyes, a very dark hazel, were not particularly large, but rather heavily freighted in their melancholy lids with sleeping passion; her nose was of that unimportant character which no man remembers; her mouth was small and straight; her teeth, white and regular. The whole expression of her face was piquancy that might be subdued by tenderness or made malevolent by anger. At present it was a salad in which the oil and vinegar were deftly combined. The astute feminine reader will of course understand that this is the ordinary superficial masculine criticism, and at once make up her mind both as to the character of the young lady and the competency of the critic. I only know that I rather liked her. And her functions are somewhat important in this veracious history.

She looked up, started to her feet, leveled her black brows at the intruder, but, at a sign from her uncle, showed her white teeth and spake.

It was only a sentence, and a rather common-place one at that; but if she could have put her voice upon her canvas, she might have retrieved the Garcia fortunes. For it was so musical, so tender, so sympathizing, so melodious, so replete with the graciousness of womanhood, that she seemed to have invented the language. And yet that sentence was only an exaggerated form of the 'How d'ye do,' whined out, doled out, lisped out, or shot out from the pretty mouths of my fair countrywomen.

Miguel admired the paintings. He was struck particularly with a crayon drawing of a mule. "Mother of God, it is the mule itself! observe how it will not go." Then the crafty Victor broke in with, "But it is nothing to her writing; look, you shall tell to me which is the handwriting of Pio Pico;" and, from a drawer in the secretary, he drew forth two signatures. One was affixed to a yellowish paper, the other drawn on plain white foolscap. Of course Miguel took the more modern one with lover-like gallantry. "It is this is genuine!" Victor laughed triumphantly; Carmen echoed the laugh melodiously in child-like glee, and added, with a slight toss of her piquant head, "It is mine!" The best of the sex will not refuse a just and overdue compliment from even the man they dislike. It's the principle they're after, not the sentiment.

But Victor was not satisfied with this proof of his niece's skill. "Say to her," he demanded of Miguel, "what name thou likest, and it shall be done before thee here." Miguel was not so much in love but he perceived the drift of Victor's suggestion, and remarked that the rubric of Governor Micheltorena was exceedingly complicated and difficult. "She shall do it!" responded Victor, with decision.

From a file of old departmental papers the Governor's signature and that involved rubric, which must have cost his late Excellency many youthful days of anxiety, was produced and laid before Carmen.

Carmen took her pen in her hand, looked at the brownish-looking document, and then at the virgin whiteness of the foolscap before her. "But," she said, pouting prettily, "I should have to first paint this white paper brown. And it will absorb the ink more quickly than that. When I painted the San Antonio of the Mission San Gabriel for Father Acolti, I had to put the decay in with my oils and brushes before the good Padre would accept it."

The two scamps looked at each other. It was their supreme moment. "I think I have," said Victor, with assumed careless-ness, "I think I have some of the old Custom-House paper." He produced from the secretary a sheet of brown paper with a stamp. "Try it on that."

Carmen smiled with childish delight, tried it, and produced a marvel! "It is as magic," said Miguel, feigning to cross himself.

Victor's role was more serious. He affected to be deeply touched, took the paper, folded it, and placed it in his breast. "I shall make a good fool of Don Jose Castro," he said; "he will declare it is the Governor's own signature, for he was his friend; but have a care, Carmen! that you spoil it not by the opening of your red lips. When he is fooled, I will tell him of this marvel,—this niece of mine, and he shall buy her pictures. Eh, little one?" and he gave her the avuncular caress, i. e., a pat of the hand on either cheek, and a kiss. Miguel envied him, but cupidity outgeneraled Cupid, and presently the conversation flagged, until a convenient recollection of Victor's—that himself and comrade were due at the Posada del Toros at 10 o'clock—gave them the opportunity to retire. But not without a chance shot from Carmen. "Tell to me," she said, half to Victor and half to Miguel, "what has chanced with Concho? He was ever ready to bring to me flowers from the mountain, and insects and birds. Thou knowest how he would sit, oh, my uncle, and talk to me of the rare rocks he had seen, and the bears and the evil spirits, and now he comes no longer, my Concho! How is this? Nothing evil has befallen him, surely?" and her drooping lids closed half-pathetically.

Miguel's jealousy took fire. "He is drunk, Senorita, doubtless, and has forgotten not only thee but, mayhap, his mule and pack! It is his custom, ha! ha!"

The red died out of Carmen's ripe lips, and she shut them together with a snap like a steel purse. The dove had suddenly changed to a hawk; the child-girl into an antique virago; the spirit hitherto dimly outlined in her face, of some shrewish Garcia ancestress, came to the fore. She darted a quick look at her uncle, and then, with her little hands on her rigid lips, strode with two steps up to Miguel.

"Possibly, O Senor Miguel Dominguez Perez (a profound courtesy here), it is as thou sayest. Drunkard Concho may be; but, drunk or sober, he never turned his back on his friend—or—(the words grated a little here)—his enemy."

Miguel would have replied, but Victor was ready. "Fool," he said, pinching his arm, "'tis an old friend. And—and—the application is still to be filled up. Are you crazy?"

But on this point Miguel was not, and with the revenge of a rival added to his other instincts, he permitted Victor to lead him away.

On their return to the fonda, they found Master Manuel too far gone with aguardiente, and a general animosity to the average Americano, to be of any service. So they worked alone, with pen, ink, and paper, in the stuffy, cigarrito-clouded back room of the fonda. It was midnight, two hours after Concho had started, that Miguel clapped spurs to his horse for the village of Tres Pinos, with an application to Governor Micheltorena for a grant to the "Rancho of the Red Rocks" comfortably bestowed in his pocket.

CHAPTER VII

WHO PLEAD FOR IT

There can be little doubt the coroner's jury of Fresno would have returned a verdict of "death from alcoholism," as the result of their inquest into the cause of Concho's death, had not Dr. Guild fought nobly in support of the law and his own convictions. A majority of the jury objected to there being any inquest at all. A sincere juryman thought it hard that whenever a Greaser pegged out in a sneakin' kind o' way, American citizens should be taken from their business to find out what ailed him. "S'pose he was killed," said another, "thar ain't no time this thirty year he weren't, so to speak, just sufferin' for it, ez his nat'ral right ez a Mexican." The jury at last compromised by bringing in a verdict of homicide against certain parties unknown. Yet it was understood tacitly that these unknown parties were severally Wiles and Pedro; Manuel, Miguel, and Roscommon proving an unmistakable alibi. Wiles and Pedro had fled to lower California, and Manuel, Miguel, and Roscommon deemed it advisable, in the then excited state of the public mind, to withhold the forged application and claim from the courts and the public comment. So that for a year after the murder of Concho and the flight of his assassins "The Blue Mass Mining Company" remained in undisturbed and actual possession of the mine, and reigned in their stead.

But the spirit of the murdered Concho would not down any more than that of the murdered Banquo, and so wrought, no doubt, in a quiet, Concho-like way, sore trouble with the "Blue Mass Company." For a great Capitalist and Master of Avarice came down to the mine and found it fair, and taking one of the Company aside, offered to lend his name and a certain amount of coin for a controlling interest, accompanying the generous offer with a suggestion that if it were not acceded to he would be compelled to buy up various Mexican mines and flood the market with quicksilver to the great detriment of the "Blue Mass Company," which thoughtful suggestion, offered by a man frequently alluded to as one of "California's great mining princes," and as one who had "done much to develop the resources of the State," was not to be lightly considered; and so, after a cautious non-consultation with the Company, and a commendable secrecy, the stockholder sold out. Whereat it was speedily spread abroad that the great Capitalist had taken hold of "Blue Mass," and the stock went up, and the other stockholders rejoiced—until the great Capitalist found that it was necessary to put up expensive mills, to employ a high salaried Superintendent, in fact, to develop the mine by the spending of its earnings, so that the stock quoted at 112 was finally saddled with an assessment of $50 per share. Another assessment of $50 to enable the Superintendent to proceed to Russia and Spain and examine into the workings of the quicksilver mines there, and also a general commission to the gifted and scientific Pillageman to examine into the various component parts of quicksilver, and report if it could not be manufactured from ordinary sand-stone by steam or electricity, speedily brought the other stockholders to their senses. It was at this time the good fellow "Tom," the serious-minded "Dick," and the speculative but fortunate "Harry," brokers of the Great Capitalist, found it convenient to buy up, for the Great Capitalist aforesaid, the various other shares at great sacrifice.

I fear that I have bored my readers in thus giving the tiresome details of that ingenuous American pastime which my countrymen dismiss in their epigrammatic way as the "freezing-out process." And lest any reader should question the ethics of the proceeding, I beg him to remember that one gentleman accomplished in this art was always a sincere and direct opponent of the late Mr. John Oakhurst, gambler.

But for once the Great Master of Avarice had not taken into sufficient account the avarice of others, and was suddenly and virtuously shocked to learn that an application for a patent for certain lands, known as the "Red-Rock Rancho," was about to be offered before the United States Land Commission. This claim covered his mining property. But the information came quietly and secretly, as all of the Great Master's information was obtained, and he took the opportunity to sell out his clouded title and his proprietorship to the only remaining member of the original "Blue Mass Company," a young fellow of pith, before many-tongued rumor had voiced the news far and wide. The blow was a heavy one to the party left in possession. Saddled by the enormous debts and expenses of the Great Capitalist, with a credit now further injured by the defection of this lucky magnate, who was admired for his skill in anticipating a loss, and whose relinquishment of any project meant ruin to it, the single-handed, impoverished possessor of the mine, whose title was contested, and whose reputation was yet to be made,—poor Biggs, first secretary and only remaining officer of the "Blue Mass Company," looked ruefully over his books and his last transfer, and sighed. But I have before intimated that he was built of good stuff, and that he believed in his work,—which was well,—and in himself, which was better; and so, having faith even as a grain of mustard seed, I doubt not he would have been able to remove that mountain of quicksilver beyond the overlapping of fraudulent grants. And, again, Providence—having disposed of these several scamps—raised up to him a friend. But that friend is of sufficient importance to this veracious history to deserve a paragraph to himself.

The Pylades of this Orestes was known of ordinary mortals as Royal Thatcher. His genealogy, birth, and education are, I take it, of little account to this chronicle, which is only concerned with his friendship for Biggs and the result thereof. He had known Biggs a year or two previously; they had shared each other's purses, bunks, cabins, provisions, and often friends, with that perfect freedom from obligation which belonged to the pioneer life. The varying tide of fortune had just then stranded Thatcher on a desert sand hill in San Francisco, with an uninsured cargo of Expectations, while to Thatcher's active but not curious fancy it had apparently lifted his friend's bark over the bar in the Monterey mountains into an open quicksilver sea. So that he was considerably surprised on receiving a note from Biggs to this purport:

"DEAR ROY—Run down here and help a fellow. I've too much of a load for one. Maybe we can make a team and pull 'Blue Mass' out yet. BIGGSEY."

Thatcher, sitting in his scantily furnished lodgings, doubtful of his next meal and in arrears for rent, heard this Macedonian cry as St. Paul did. He wrote a promissory and soothing note to his landlady, but fearing the "sweet sorrow" of personal parting, let his collapsed valise down from his window by a cord, and, by means of an economical combination of stage riding and pedestrianism, he presented himself, at the close of the third day, at Biggs's door. In a few moments he was in possession of the story; half an hour later in possession of half the mine, its infelix past and its doubtful future, equally with his friend.

Business over, Biggs turned to look at his partner. "You've aged some since I saw you last," he said. "Starvation luck, I s'pose. I'd know your eyes, old fellow, if I saw them among ten thousand; but your lips are parched, and your mouth's grimmer than it used to be." Thatcher smiled to show that he could still do so, but did not say, as he might have said, that self-control, suppressed resentment, disappointment, and occasional hunger had done something in the way of correcting Nature's obvious mistakes, and shutting up a kindly mouth. He only took off his threadbare coat, rolled up his sleeves, and saying, "We've got lots of work and some fighting before us," pitched into the "affairs" of the "Blue Mass Company" on the instant.

CHAPTER VIII

OF COUNSEL FOR IT

Meanwhile Roscommon had waited. Then, in Garcia's name, and backed by him, he laid his case before the Land Commissioner, filing the application (with forged indorsements) to Governor Micheltorena, and alleging that the original grant was destroyed by fire. And why?

It seemed there was a limit to Miss Carmen's imitative talent. Admirable as it was, it did not reach to the reproduction of that official seal, which would have been a necessary appendage to the Governor's grant. But there were letters written on stamped paper by Governor Micheltorena to himself, Garcia, and to Miguel, and to Manuel's father, all of which were duly signed by the sign manual and rubric of Mrs.-Governor-Micheltorena-Carmen-de-Haro. And then there was "parol" evidence, and plenty of it; witnesses who remembered everything about it,—namely, Manuel, Miguel, and the all-recollecting De Haro; here were details, poetical and suggestive; and Dame-Quicklyish, as when his late Excellency, sitting not "by a sea-coal fire," but with aguardiente and cigarros, had sworn to him, the ex-ecclesiastic Miguel, that he should grant, and had granted, Garcia's request. There were clouds of witnesses, conversations, letters, and records, glib and pat to the occasion. In brief, there was nothing wanted but the seal of his Excellency. The only copy of that was in the possession of a rival school of renaissant art and the restoration of antiques, then doing business before the Land Commission.

And yet the claim was rejected! Having lately recommended two separate claimants to a patent for the same land, the Land Commission became cautious and conservative.

Roscommon was at first astounded, then indignant, and then warlike,—he was for an "appale to onst!"

With the reader's previous knowledge of Roscommon's disposition this may seem somewhat inconsistent; but there are certain natures to whom litigation has all the excitement of gambling, and it should be borne in mind that this was his first lawsuit. So that his lawyer, Mr. Saponaceous Wood, found him in that belligerent mood to which counsel are obliged to hypocritically bring all the sophistries of their profession.

"Of course you have your right to an appeal, but calm yourself, my dear sir, and consider. The case was presented strongly, the evidence overwhelming on our side, but we happened to be fighting previous decisions of the Land Commission that had brought them into trouble; so that if Micheltorena had himself appeared in Court and testified to his giving you the grant, it would have made no difference,—no Spanish grant had a show then, nor will it have for the next six months. You see, my dear sir, the Government sent out one of its big Washington lawyers to look into this business, and he reported frauds, sir, frauds, in a majority of the Spanish claims. And why, sir? why? He was bought, sir, bought—body and soul—by the Ring!"

"And fwhot's the Ring?" asked his client sharply.

"The Ring is—ahem! a combination of unprincipled but wealthy persons to defeat the ends of justice."

"And sure, fwhot's the Ring to do wid me grant as that thaving Mexican gave me as the collatherals for the bourd he was owin' me? Eh, mind that now!"

"The Ring, my dear sir, is the other side. It is—ahem! always the Other Side."

"And why the divel haven't we a Ring too? And ain't I payin' ye five hundred dollars,—and the divel of Ring ye have, at all, at all? Fwhot am I payin' ye fur, eh?"

"That a judicious expenditure of money," began Mr. Wood, "outside of actual disbursements, may not be of infinite service to you I am not prepared to deny,—but—"

"Look ye, Mr. Sappy Wood, it's the 'appale' I want, and the grant I'll have, more betoken as the old woman's har-rut and me own is set on it entoirely. Get me the land and I'll give ye the half of it,—and it's a bargain!"

"But my dear sir, there are some rules in our profession,—technical though they may be—"

"The divel fly away wid yer profession. Sure is it better nor me own? If I've risked me provisions and me whisky, that cost me solid goold in Frisco, on that thafe Garcia's claim, bedad! the loikes of ye can risk yer law."

"Well," said Wood, with an awkward smile, "I suppose that a deed for one half, on the consideration of friendship, my dear sir, and a dollar in hand paid by me, might be reconcilable."

"Now it's talkin' ye are. But who's the felly we're foighten, that's got the Ring?"

"Ah, my dear sir, it's the United States," said the lawyer with gravity.

"The States! the Government is it? And is't that ye're afeared of? Sure it's the Government that I fought in me own counthree, it was the Government that druv me to Ameriky, and is it now that I'm going back on me principles?"

"Your political sentiments do you great credit," began Mr. Wood.

"But fwhot's the Government to do wid the appale?"

"The Government," said Mr. Wood significantly, "will be represented by the District Attorney."

"And who's the spalpeen?"

"It is rumored," said Mr. Wood, slowly, "that a new one is to be appointed. I, myself, have had some ambition that way."

His client bent a pair of cunning but not over-wise grey eyes on his American lawyer. But he only said, "Ye have, eh?"

"Yes," said Wood, answering the look boldly; "and if I had the support of a number of your prominent countrymen, who are so powerful with ALL parties,—men like YOU, my dear sir,—why, I think you might in time become a conservative, at least more resigned to the Government."

Then the lesser and the greater scamp looked at each other, and for a moment or two felt a warm, sympathetic, friendly emotion for each other, and quietly shook hands.

Depend upon it there is a great deal more kindly human sympathy between two openly-confessed scamps than there is in that calm, respectable recognition that you and I, dear reader, exhibit when we happen to oppose each other with our respective virtues.

"And ye'll get the appale?"

"I will."

And he DID! And by a singular coincidence got the District Attorneyship also. And with a deed for one half of the "Red-Rock Rancho" in his pocket, sent a brother lawyer in court to appear for his client, the United States, as against HIMSELF, Roscommon, Garcia, et al. Wild horses could not have torn him from this noble resolution. There is an indescribable delicacy in the legal profession which we literary folk ought to imitate.

The United States lost! Which meant ruin and destruction to the "Blue Mass Company," who had bought from a paternal and beneficent Government lands which didn't belong to it. The Mexican grant, of course, antedated the occupation of the mine by Concho, Wiles, Pedro, et al., as well as by the "Blue Mass Company," and the solitary partners, Biggs and Thatcher. More than that, it swallowed up their improvements. It made Biggs and Thatcher responsible to Garcia for all the money the Grand Master of Avarice had made out of it. Mr. District Attorney was apparently distressed, but resigned. Messrs. Biggs and Thatcher were really distressed and combative.

And then, to advance a few years in this chronicle, began real litigation with earnestness, vigor, courage, zeal, and belief on the part of Biggs and Thatcher, and technicalities, delay, equivocation, and a general Fabian-like policy on the part of Garcia, Roscommon, et al. Of all these tedious processes I note but one, which for originality and audacity of conception appears to me to indicate more clearly the temper and civilization of the epoch. A subordinate officer of the District Court refused to obey the mandate ordering a transcript of the record to be sent up to the United States Supreme Court. It is to be regretted that the name of this Ephesian youth, who thus fired the dome of our constitutional liberties, should have been otherwise so unimportant as to be confined to the dusty records of that doubtful court of which he was a doubtful servitor, and that his claim to immortality ceased with his double-feed service. But there still stands on record a letter by this young gentleman, arraigning the legal wisdom of the land, which is not entirely devoid of amusement or even instruction to young men desirous of obtaining publicity and capital. Howbeit, the Supreme Court was obliged to protect itself by procuring the legislation of his functions out of his local fingers into the larger palm of its own attorney.

These various processes of law and equity, which, when exercised practically in the affairs of ordinary business, might have occupied a few months' time, dragged, clung, retrograded, or advanced slowly during a period of eight or nine years. But the strong arms of Biggs and Thatcher held POSSESSION, and possibly, by the same tactics employed on the other side, arrested or delayed ejectment, and so made and sold quicksilver, while their opponents were spending gold, until Biggs, sorely hit in the interlacings of his armor, fell in the lists, his cheek growing waxen and his strong arm feeble, and finding himself in this sore condition, and passing, as it were, made over his share in trust to his comrade, and died. Whereat, from that time henceforward, Royal Thatcher reigned in his stead.

And so, having anticipated the legal record, we will go back to the various human interests that helped to make it up.

To begin with Roscommon: To do justice to his later conduct and expressions, it must be remembered that when he accepted the claim for the "Red-Rock Rancho," yet unquestioned, from the hands of Garcia, he was careless, or at least unsuspicious of fraud. It was not until he had experienced the intoxication of litigation that he felt, somehow, that he was a wronged and defrauded man, but with the obstinacy of defrauded men, preferred to arraign some one fact or individual as the impelling cause of his wrong, rather than the various circumstances that led to it. To his simple mind it was made patent that the "Blue Mass Company" were making money out of a mine which he claimed, and which was not yet adjudged to them. Every dollar they took out was a fresh count in this general indictment. Every delay towards this adjustment of rights—although made by his own lawyer—was a personal wrong. The mere fact that there never was nor had been any quid pro quo for this immense property—that it had fallen to him for a mere song—only added zest to his struggle. The possibility of his losing this mere speculation affected him more strongly than if he had already paid down the million he expected to get from the mine. I don't know that I have indicated as plainly as I might that universal preference on the part of mankind to get something from nothing, and to acquire the largest return for the least possible expenditure, but I question my right to say that Roscommon was much more reprehensible than his fellows.

But it told upon him as it did upon all over whom the spirit of the murdered Concho brooded,—upon all whom avarice alternately flattered and tortured. From his quiet gains in his legitimate business, from the little capital accumulated through industry and economy, he lavished thousands on this chimera of his fancy. He grew grizzled and worn over his self-imposed delusion; he no longer jested with his customers, regardless of quality or station or importance; he had cliques to mollify, enemies to placate, friends to reward. The grocery suffered; through giving food and lodgment to clouds of unimpeachable witnesses before the Land Commission and the District Court, "Mrs. Ros." found herself losing money. Even the bar failed; there was a party of "Blue Mass" employees who drank at the opposite fonda, and cursed the Roscommon claim over the liquor. The calm, mechanical indifference with which Roscommon had served his customers was gone. The towel was no longer used after its perfunctory fashion; the counter remained unwiped; the disks of countless glasses marked its surface, and indicated other preoccupation on the part of the proprietor. The keen grey eyes of the claimant of the "Red-Rock Rancho" were always on the lookout for friend or enemy.

Garcia comes next. That gentleman's inborn talent for historic misrepresentation culminated unpleasantly through a defective memory; a year or two after he had sworn in his application for the "Rancho," being engaged in another case, some trifling inconsistency was discovered in his statements, which had the effect of throwing the weight of evidence to the party who had paid him most, but was instantly detected by the weaker party. Garcia's preeminence as a witness, an expert and general historian began to decline. He was obliged to be corroborated, and this required a liberal outlay of his fee. With the loss of his credibility as a witness bad habits supervened. He was frequently drunk, he lost his position, he lost his house, and Carmen, removed to San Francisco, supported him with her brush.

And this brings us once more to that pretty painter and innocent forger whose unconscious act bore such baleful fruit on the barren hill-sides of the "Red-Rock Rancho," and also to a later blossom of her life, that opened, however, in kindlier sunshine.

CHAPTER IX

WHAT THE FAIR HAD TO DO ABOUT IT

The house that Royal Thatcher so informally quitted in his exodus to the promised land of Biggs was one of those oversized, under-calculated dwellings conceived and erected in the extravagance of the San Francisco builder's hopes, and occupied finally in his despair. Intended originally as the palace of some inchoate California Aladdin, it usually ended as a lodging house in which some helpless widow or hopeless spinster managed to combine respectability with the hard task of bread getting.

Thatcher's landlady was one of the former class. She had unfortunately survived not only her husband but his property, and, living in some deserted chamber, had, after the fashion of the Italian nobility, let out the rest of the ruin. A tendency to dwell upon these facts gave her conversation a peculiar significance on the first of each month. Thatcher had noticed this with the sensitiveness of an impoverished gentleman. But when, a few days after her lodger's sudden disappearance, a note came from him containing a draft in noble excess of all arrears and charges, the widow's heart was lifted, and the rock smitten with the golden wand gushed beneficence that shone in a new gown for the widow and a new suit for "Johnny," her son, a new oil cloth in the hall, better service to the lodgers, and, let us be thankful, a kindlier consideration for the poor little black-eyed painter from Monterey, then dreadfully behind in her room rent. For, to tell the truth, the calls upon Miss De Haro's scant purse by her uncle had lately been frequent, perjury having declined in the Monterey market, through excessive and injudicious supply, until the line of demarcation between it and absolute verity was so finely drawn that Victor Garcia had remarked that "he might as well tell the truth at once and save his soul, since the devil was in the market."

Mistress Plodgitt, the landlady, could not resist the desire to acquaint Carmen De Haro with her good fortune. "He was always a friend of yours, my dear,—and I know him to be a gentleman that would never let a poor widow suffer; and see what he says about you!" Here she produced Thatcher's note and read: "Tell my little neighbor that I shall come back soon to carry her and her sketching tools off by force, and I shall not let her return until she has caught the black mountains and the red rocks she used to talk about, and put the 'Blue Mass' mill in the foreground of the picture I shall order."

What is this, little one? Surely, Carmen, thou needst not blush at this, thy first grand offer. Holy Virgin! is it of a necessity that thou shouldst stick the wrong end of thy brush in thy mouth, and then drop it in thy lap? Or was it taught thee by the good Sisters at the convent to stride in that boyish fashion to the side of thy elders and snatch from their hands the missive thou wouldst read? More of this we would know, O Carmen,—smallest of brunettes,—speak, little one, even in thine own melodious speech, that I may commend thee and thy rare discretion to my own fair countrywomen.

Alas, neither the present chronicler nor Mistress Plodgitt got any further information from the prudent Carmen, and must fain speculate upon certain facts that were already known.

Mistress Carmen's little room was opposite to Thatcher's, and once or twice, the doors being open, Thatcher had a glimpse across the passage of a black-haired and a sturdy, boyish little figure in a great blue apron, perched on a stool before an easel, and on the other hand, Carmen had often been conscious of the fumes of a tobacco pipe penetrating her cloistered seclusion, and had seen across the passage, vaguely enveloped in the same nicotine cloud, an American Olympian, in a rocking chair, with his feet on the mantel shelf. They had once or twice met on the staircase, on which occasion Thatcher had greeted her with a word or two of respectful yet half-humorous courtesy,—a courtesy which never really offends a true woman, although it often piques her self-aplomb by the slight assumption of superiority in the humorist. A woman is quick to recognize the fact that the great and more dangerous passions are always SERIOUS, and may be excused if in self-respect she is often induced to try if there be not somewhere under the skin of this laughing Mercutio the flesh and blood of a Romeo. Thatcher was by nature a defender and protector; weakness, and weakness alone, stirred the depths of his tenderness,—often, I fear, only through its half-humorous aspects,—and on this plane he was pleased to place women and children. I mention this fact for the benefit of the more youthful members of my species, and am satisfied that an unconditional surrender and the complete laying down at the feet of Beauty of all strong masculinity is a cheap Gallicism that is untranslatable to most women worthy the winning. For a woman MUST always look up to the man she truly loves,—even if she has to go down on her knees to do it.

Only the masculine reader will infer from this that Carmen was in love with Thatcher; the more critical and analytical feminine eye will see nothing herein that might not have happened consistently with friendship. For Thatcher was no sentimentalist; he had hardly paid a compliment to the girl,—even in the unspoken but most delicate form of attention. There were days when his room door was closed; there were days succeeding these blanks when he met her as frankly and naturally as if he had seen her yesterday. Indeed, on those days following his flight the simple-minded Carmen, being aware—heaven knows how—that he had not opened his door during that period, and fearing sickness, sudden death, or perhaps suicide, by her appeals to the landlady, assisted unwittingly in discovering his flight and defection. As she was for a few moments as indignant as Mrs. Plodgitt, it is evident that she had but little sympathy with the delinquent. And besides, hitherto she had known only Concho, her earliest friend, and was true to his memory, as against all Americanos, whom she firmly believed to be his murderers.

So she dismissed the offer and the man from her mind, and went back to her painting,—a fancy portrait of the good Padre Junipero Serra, a great missionary, who, haply for the integrity of his bones and character, died some hundred years before the Americans took possession of California. The picture was fair but unsaleable, and she began to think seriously of sign painting, which was then much more popular and marketable. An unfinished head of San Juan de Bautista, artificially framed in clouds, she disposed of to a prominent druggist for $50, where it did good service as exhibiting the effect of four bottles of "Jones's Freckle Eradicator," and in a pleasant and unobtrusive way revived the memory of the saint. Still, she felt weary and was growing despondent, and had a longing for the good Sisters and the blameless lethargy of conventual life, and then—

He came!

But not as the Prince should come, on a white charger, to carry away this cruelly-abused and enchanted damsel. He was sunburned, he was bearded like "the pard"; he was a little careless as to his dress, and pre-occupied in his ways. But his mouth and eyes were the same; and when he repeated in his old frank, half-mischievous way the invitation of his letter, poor little Carmen could only hesitate and blush.

A thought struck him and sent the color to his face. Your gentleman born is always as modest as a woman. He ran down stairs, and seizing the widowed Plodgitt, said hastily:

"You're just killing yourself here. Take a change. Come down to Monterey for a day or two with me, and bring miss De Haro with you for company."

The old lady recognized the situation. Thatcher was now a man of vast possibilities. In all maternal daughters of Eve there is the slightest bit of the chaperone and match-maker. It is the last way of reviving the past.

She consented, and Carmen De Haro could not well refuse.

The ladies found the "Blue Mass" mills very much as Thatcher had previously delivered it to them, "a trifle rough and mannish." But he made over to them the one tenement reserved for himself, and slept with his men, or more likely under the trees. At first Mrs. Plodgitt missed gas and running water, and these several conveniences of civilization, among which I fear may be mentioned sheets and pillow cases; but the balsam of the mountain air soothed her neuralgia and her temper. As for Carmen, she rioted in the unlimited license of her absolute freedom from conventional restraint and the indulgence of her child-like impulses. She scoured the ledges far and wide alone; she dipped into dark copses, and scrambled over sterile patches of chemisal, and came back laden with the spoil of buckeye blossoms, manzanita berries and laurel. But she would not make a sketch of the "Blue

Mass Company's" mills on a Mercator's projection—something that could be afterwards lithographed or chromoed, with the mills turning out tons of quicksilver through the energies of a happy and picturesque assemblage of miners— even to please her padrone, Don Royal Thatcher. On the contrary, she made a study of the ruins of the crumbled and decayed red-rock furnace, with the black mountain above it, and the light of a dying camp fire shining upon it, and the dull-red excavations in the ledge. But even this did not satisfy her until she had made some alterations; and when she finally brought her finished study to Don Royal, she looked at him a little defiantly. Thatcher admired honestly, and then criticised a little humorously and dishonestly. "But couldn't you, for a consideration, put up a sign-board on that rock with the inscription, 'Road to the Blue Mass Company's new mills to the right,' and combine business with art? That's the fault of you geniuses. But what's this blanketed figure doing here, lying before the furnace? You never saw one of my miners there,—and a Mexican, too, by his serape." "That," quoth Mistress Carmen, coolly, "was put in to fill up the foreground,—I wanted something there to balance the picture." "But," continued Thatcher, dropping into unconscious admiration again, "it's drawn to the life. Tell me, Miss De Haro, before I ask the aid and counsel of Mrs. Plodgitt, who is my hated rival, and your lay figure and model?" "Oh," said Carmen, with a little sigh, "It's only poor Coucho." "And where is Concho?" (a little impatiently.) "He's dead, Don Royal." "Dead?" "Of a verity,—very dead, —murdered by your countrymen." "I see,—and you know him?" "He was my friend."

"Oh!"

"Truly."

"But" (wickedly), "isn't this a rather ghastly advertisement—

outside of an illustrated newspaper—of my property?"

"Ghastly, Don Royal. Look you, he sleeps."

"Ay" (in Spanish), "as the dead."

Carmen (crossing herself hastily), "After the fashion of the dead."

They were both feeling uncomfortable. Carmen was shivering. But, being a woman, and tactful, she recovered her head first. "It is a study for myself, Don Royal; I shall make you another."

And she slipped away, as she thought, out of the subject and his presence.

But she was mistaken; in the evening he renewed the conversation. Carmen began to fence, not from cowardice or deceit, as the masculine reader would readily infer, but from some wonderful feminine instinct that told her to be cautious. But he got from her the fact, to him before unknown, that she was the niece of his main antagonist, and, being a gentleman, so redoubled his attentions and his cour-tesy that Mrs. Plodgitt made up her mind that it was a foregone conclusion, and seriously reflected as to what she should wear on the momentous occasion. But that night poor Carmen cried herself to sleep, resolving that she would hereafter cast aside her wicked uncle for this good-hearted Americano, yet never once connected her innocent penmanship with the deadly feud between them. Women—the best of them—are strong as to collateral facts, swift of deduction, but vague as children are to the exact statement or recognition of premises. It is hardly necessary to say that Carmen had never thought of connecting any act of hers with the claims of her uncle, and the circumstance of the signature she had totally forgotten.

The masculine reader will now understand Carmen's confusion and blushes, and believe himself an ass to have thought them a confession of original affection. The feminine reader will, by this time, become satisfied that the deceitful minx's sole idea was to gain the affections of Thatcher. And really I don't know who is right.

Nevertheless she painted a sketch of Thatcher,—which now adorns the Company's office in San Francisco,—in which the property is laid out in pleasing geometrical lines, and the rosy promise of the future instinct in every touch of the brush. Then, having earned her "wage," as she believed, she became somewhat cold and shy to Thatcher. Whereat that gentleman redoubled his attentions, seeing only in her presence a certain meprise, which concerned her more than himself. The niece of his enemy meant nothing more to him than an interesting girl,—to be protected always,—to be feared, never. But even suspicion may be insidiously placed in noble minds.

Mistress Plodgitt, thus early estopped of matchmaking, of course put the blame on her own sex, and went over to the stronger side—the man's.

"It's a great pity gals should be so curious," she said, sotto voce, to Thatcher, when Carmen was in one of her sullen moods. "Yet I s'pose it's in her blood. Them Spaniards is always revengeful,—like the Eyetalians."

Thatcher honestly looked his surprise.

"Why, don't you see, she's thinking how all these lands might have been her uncle's but for you. And instead of trying to be sweet and—" here she stopped to cough.

"Good God!" said Thatcher in great concern, "I never

thought of that." He stopped for a moment, and then added with decision, "I can't believe it; it isn't like her."

Mrs. P. was piqued. She walked away, delivering, however, this Parthian arrow: "Well, I hope 'TAINT NOTHING WORSE."

Thatcher chuckled, then felt uneasy. When he next met Carmen, she found his grey eyes fixed on hers with a curious, half-inquisitorial look she had never noticed before. This only added fuel to the fire. Forgetting their relations of host and guest, she was absolutely rude. Thatcher was quiet but watchful; got the Plodgitt to bed early, and, under cover of showing a moonlight view of the "Lost Chance Mill," decoyed Carmen out of ear-shot, as far as the dismantled furnace.

"What is the matter, Miss De Haro; have I offended you?"

Miss Carmen was not aware that anything was the matter. If Don Royal preferred old friends, whose loyalty of course he knew, and who were above speaking ill against a gentleman in his adversity—(oh, Carmen! fie!) if he preferred THEIR company to LATER FRIENDS—why—(the masculine reader will observe this tremendous climax and tremble)— why she didn't know why HE should blame HER.

They turned and faced each other. The conditions for a perfect misunderstanding could not have been better arranged between two people. Thatcher was a masculine reasoner, Carmen a feminine feeler,—if I may be pardoned the expression. Thatcher wanted to get at certain facts, and argue therefrom. Carmen wanted to get at certain feelings, and then fit the facts to THEM.

"But I am NOT blaming you, Miss Carmen," he said gravely.

"It WAS stupid in me to confront you here with the property claimed by your uncle and occupied by me, but it was a mistake,—no!" he added hastily, "it was not a mistake. You knew it, and I didn't. You overlooked it before you came, and I was too glad to overlook it after you were here."

"Of course," said Carmen pettishly, "I am the only one to be blamed. It's like you MEN!" (Mem. She was just fifteen, and uttered this awful 'resume' of experience just as if it hadn't been taught to her in her cradle.)

Feminine generalities always stagger a man. Thatcher said nothing. Carmen became more enraged.

"Why did you want to take Uncle Victor's property, then?" she asked triumphantly.

"I don't know that it is your uncle's property."

"You—don't—know? Have you seen the application with Governor Micheltorena's indorsement? Have you heard the witnesses?" she said passionately.

"Signatures may be forged and witnesses lie," said Thatcher quietly.

"What is it you call 'forged'?"

Thatcher instantly recalled the fact that the Spanish language held no synonym for "forgery." The act was apparently an invention of el Diablo Americano. So he said, with a slight smile in his kindly eyes:

"Anybody wicked enough and dexterous enough can imitate another's handwriting. When this is used to benefit fraud, we call it 'forgery.' I beg your pardon,—Miss De Haro, Miss

Carmen,—what is the matter?"

She had suddenly lapsed against a tree, quite helpless, nerveless, and with staring eyes fixed on his. As yet an embryo woman, inexperienced and ignorant, the sex's instinct was potential; she had in one plunge fathomed all that his reason had been years groping for.

Thatcher saw only that she was pained, that she was helpless: that was enough. "It is possible that your uncle may have been deceived," he began; "many honest men have been fooled by clever but deceitful tricksters, men and women—"

"Stop! Madre de Dios! WILL YOU STOP?"

Thatcher for an instant recoiled from the flashing eyes and white face of the little figure that had, with menacing and clenched baby fingers, strode to his side. He stopped. "Where is this application,—this forgery?" she asked. "Show it to me!"

Thatcher felt relieved, and smiled the superior smile of our sex over feminine ignorance. "You could hardly expect me to be trusted with your uncle's vouchers. His papers of course are in the hands of his counsel."

"And when can I leave this place?" she asked passionately.

"If you consult my wishes you will stay, if only long enough to forgive me. But if I have offended you unknowingly, and you are implacable—"

"I can go to-morrow at sunrise if I like?"

"As you will," returned Thatcher gravely.

"Gracias, Senor."

They walked slowly back to the house, Thatcher with a masculine sense of being unreasonably afflicted, Carmen with a woman's instinct of being hopelessly crushed. No word was spoken until they reached the door. Then Carmen suddenly, in her old, impulsive way, and in a childlike treble, sang out merrily, "Good night, O Don Royal, and pleasant dreams. Hasta manana."

Thatcher stood dumb and astounded at this capricious girl. She saw his mystification instantly. "It is for the old Cat!" she whispered, jerking her thumb over her shoulder in the direction of the sleeping Mrs. P. "Good night,—go!"

He went to give orders for a peon to attend the ladies and their equipage the next day. He awoke to find Miss De Haro gone, with her escort, towards Monterey. And without the Plodgitt.

He could not conceal his surprise from the latter lady. She, left alone,—a not altogether unavailable victim to the wiles of our sex,—was embarrassed. But not so much that she could not say to Thatcher: "I told you so,—gone to her uncle. . . . To tell him ALL!"

"All. D—n it, WHAT can she tell him?" roared Thatcher, stung out of his self-control.

"Nothing, I hope, that she should not," said Mrs. P., and chastely retired.

She was right. Miss Carmen posted to Monterey, running her horse nearly off its legs to do it, and then sent back her beast and escort, saying she would rejoin Mrs. Plodgitt by steamer at San Francisco. Then she went boldly to the law office of

Saponaceous Wood, District Attorney and whilom solicitor of her uncle.

With the majority of masculine Monterey Miss Carmen was known and respectfully admired, despite the infelix reputation of her kinsman. Mr. Wood was glad to see her, and awkwardly gallant. Miss Carmen was cool and business-like; she had come from her uncle to "regard" the papers in the "Red-Rock Rancho" case. They were instantly produced. Carmen turned to the application for the grant. Her cheek paled slightly. With her clear memory and wonderful fidelity of perception she could not be mistaken. THE SIGNATURE OF MICHELTORENA WAS IN HER OWN HANDWRITING!

Yet she looked up to the lawyer with a smile: "May I take these papers for an hour to my uncle?"

Even an older and better man than the District Attorney could not have resisted those drooping lids and that gentle voice.

"Certainly."

"I will return them in an hour."

She was as good as her word, and within the hour dropped the papers and a little courtesy to her uncle's legal advocate, and that night took the steamer to San Francisco.

The next morning Victor Garcia, a little the worse for the previous night's dissipation, reeled into Wood's office. "I have fears for my niece Carmen. She is with the enemy," he said thickly. "Look you at this."

It was an anonymous letter (in Mrs. Plodgitt's own awkward

fist) advising him of the fact that his niece was bought by the enemy, and cautioning him against her.

"Impossible," said the lawyer; "it was only last week she sent thee $50."

Victor blushed, even through his ensanguined cheeks, and made an impatient gesture with his hand.

"Besides," added the lawyer coolly, "she has been here to examine the papers at thy request, and returned them of yesterday."

Victor gasped: "And-you-you-gave them to her?"

"Of course!"

"All? Even the application and the signature?"

"Certainly,—you sent her."

"Sent her? The devil's own daughter?" shrieked Garcia. "No! A hundred million times, no! Quick, before it is too late. Give to me the papers."

Mr. Wood reproduced the file. Garcia ran over it with trembling fingers until at last he clutched the fateful document. Not content with opening it and glancing at its text and signature, he took it to the window.

"It is the same," he muttered with a sigh of relief.

"Of course it is," said Mr. Wood sharply. "The papers are all there. You're a fool, Victor Garcia!"

And so he was. And, for the matter of that, so was Mr.

Saponaceous Wood, of counsel.

Meanwhile Miss De Haro returned to San Francisco and resumed her work. A day or two later she was joined by her landlady. Mrs. P. had too large a nature to permit an anonymous letter, written by her own hand, to stand between her and her demeanor to her little lodger. So she coddled her and flattered her and depicted in slightly exaggerated colors the grief of Don Royal at her sudden departure. All of which Miss Carmen received in a demure, kitten-like way, but still kept quietly at her work. In due time Don Royal's order was completed; still she had leisure and inclination enough to add certain touches to her ghastly sketch of the crumbling furnace.

Nevertheless, as Don Royal did not return, through excess of business, Mrs. Plodgitt turned an honest penny by letting his room, temporarily, to two quiet Mexicans, who, but for a beastly habit of cigarrito smoking which tainted the whole house, were fair enough lodgers. If they failed in making the acquaintance of their fair countrywoman, Miss De Haro, it was through the lady's pre-occupation in her own work, and not through their ostentatious endeavors.

"Miss De Haro is peculiar," explained the politic Mrs. Plodgitt to her guests; "she makes no acquaintances, which I consider bad for her business. If it had not been for me, she would not have known Royal Thatcher, the great quicksilver miner,—and had his order for a picture of his mine!"

The two foreign gentlemen exchanged glances. One said, "Ah, God! this is bad," and the other, "It is not possible;" and then, when the landlady's back was turned, introduced themselves with a skeleton key into the then vacant bedroom and studio of their fair countrywoman, who was absent sketching. "Thou observest," said Mr. Pedro, refugee, to Miguel, ex-ecclesiastic, "that this Americano is all-powerful, and that this Victor, drunkard as he is, is right in his suspicions."

"Of a verity, yes," replied Miguel, "thou dost remember it was Jovita Castro who, for her Americano lover, betrayed the Sobriente claim. It is only with us, my Pedro, that the Mexican spirit, the real God and Liberty, yet lives!"

They shook hands nobly and with sentimental fervor, and then went to work, i. e., the rummaging over the trunks, drawers, and portmanteaus of the poor little painter, Carmen de Haro, and even ripped up the mattress of her virginal cot. But they found not what they sought.

"What is that yonder on the easel, covered with a cloth?" said Miguel: "it is a trick of these artists to put their valuables together."

Pedro strode to the easel and tore away the muslin curtain that veiled it; then uttered a shriek that appalled his comrade and brought him to his side.

"In the name of God," said Miguel hastily, "are you trying to alarm the house?"

The ex-vaquero was trembling like a child. "Look," he said hoarsely, "look, do you see? It is the hand of God," and fainted on the floor!

Miguel looked. It was Carmen's partly-finished sketch of the deserted furnace. The figure of Concho, thrown out strongly by the camp fire, occupied the left foreground. But to balance her picture she had evidently been obliged to introduce another,—the face and figure of Pedro, on all fours, creeping towards the sleeping man.

PART III—IN CONGRESS

CHAPTER X

WHO LOBBIED FOR IT

It was a midsummer's day in Washington. Even at early morning, while the sun was yet level with the faces of pedestrians in its broad, shadeless avenues, it was insufferably hot. Later the avenues themselves shone like the diverging rays of another sun,—the Capitol,—a thing to be feared by the naked eye. Later yet it grew hotter, and then a mist arose from the Potomac, and blotted out the blazing arch above, and presently piled up along the horizon delusive thunder clouds, that spent their strength and substance elsewhere, and left it hotter than before. Towards evening the sun came out invigorated, having cleared the heavenly brow of perspiration, but leaving its fever unabated.

The city was deserted. The few who remained apparently buried themselves from the garish light of day in some dim, cloistered recess of shop, hotel, or restaurant; and the perspiring stranger, dazed by the outer glare, who broke in upon their quiet, sequestered repose, confronted collarless and coatless specters of the past, with fans in their hands, who, after dreamily going through some perfunctory business, immediately retired to sleep after the stranger had gone.

Congressmen and Senators had long since returned to their several constituencies with the various information that the country was going to ruin, or that the outlook never was more hopeful and cheering, as the tastes of their constituency indicated. A few Cabinet officers still lingered, having by this time become convinced that they could do nothing their own way, or indeed in any way but the old way, and getting gloomily resigned to their situation. A body of learned, cultivated men, representing the highest legal tribunal in the land, still lingered in a vague idea of earning the scant salary bestowed upon them by the economical founders of the Government, and listened patiently to the arguments of counsel, whose fees for advocacy of claims before them would have paid the life income of half the bench. There was Mr. Attorney-General and his assistants still protecting the Government's millions from rapacious hands, and drawing the yearly public pittance that their wealthier private antagonists would have scarce given as a retainer to their junior counsel. The little standing army of departmental employes,—the helpless victims of the most senseless and idiotic form of discipline the world has known,—a discipline so made up of caprice, expediency, cowardice, and tyranny that its reform meant revolution, not to be tolerated by legislators and lawgivers, or a despotism in which half a dozen accidentally-chosen men interpreted their prejudices or preferences as being that Reform. Administration after administration and Party after Party had persisted in their desperate attempts to fit the youthful colonial garments, made by our Fathers after a by-gone fashion, over the expanded limits and generous outline of a matured nation. There were patches here and there; there were grievous rents and holes here and there; there were ludicrous and painful exposures of growing limbs everywhere; and the Party in Power and the Party out of Power could do nothing but mend and patch, and revamp and cleanse and scour, and occasionally, in the wildness of despair, suggest even the cutting off the rebellious limbs that persisted in growing beyond the swaddling clothes of its infancy.

It was a capital of Contradictions and Inconsistencies. At one end of the Avenue sat the responsible High Keeper of the military honor, valor, and war-like prestige of a great nation, without the power to pay his own troops their legal dues until some selfish quarrel between Party and Party was settled. Hard by sat another Secretary, whose established functions seemed to be the misrepresentation of the nation abroad by the least characteristic of its classes, the politicians,—and only then when they had been defeated as politicians, and when their constituents had declared them no longer worthy to be even THEIR representatives. This National Absurdity was only equaled by another, wherein an ex-Politician was for four years expected to uphold the honor of a flag of a great nation over an ocean he had never tempted, with a discipline the rudiments of which he could scarcely acquire before he was removed, or his term of office expired, receiving his orders from a superior officer as ignorant of his special duties as himself, and subjected to the revision of a Congress cognizant of him only as a politician. At the farther end of the Avenue was another department so vast in its extent and so varied in its functions that few of the really great practical workers of the land would have accepted its responsibility for ten times its salary, but which the most perfect constitution in the world handed over to men who were obliged to make it a stepping stone to future preferment. There was another department, more suggestive of its financial functions from the occasional extravagances or economies exhibited in its payrolls,—successive Congresses having taken other matters out of its hands,—presided over by an official who bore the title and responsibility of the Custodian and Disburser of the Nation's Purse, and received a salary that a bank-President would have sniffed at. For it was part of this Constitutional Inconsistency and

Administrative Absurdity that in the matter of honor, justice, fidelity to trust, and even business integrity, the official was always expected to be the superior of the Government he represented. Yet the crowning Inconsistency was that, from time to time, it was submitted to the sovereign people to declare if these various Inconsistencies were not really the perfect expression of the most perfect Government the world had known. And it is to be recorded that the unanimous voices of Representative, Orator, and Unfettered Poetry were that it was!

Even the public press lent itself to the Great Inconsistency. It was as clear as crystal to the journal on one side of the Avenue that the country was going to the dogs unless the SPIRIT of the Fathers once more reanimated the public; it was equally clear to the journal on the other side of the Avenue that only a rigid adherence to the LETTER of the Fathers would save the nation from decline. It was obvious to the first-named journal that the "letter" meant Government patronage to the other journal; it was patent to that journal that the "shekels" of Senator X really animated the spirit of the Fathers. Yet all agreed it was a great and good and perfect government,—subject only to the predatory incursions of a Hydra-headed monster known as a "Ring." The Ring's origin was wrapped in secrecy, its fecundity was alarming; but although its rapacity was preternatural, its digestion was perfect and easy. It circumvolved all affairs in an atmosphere of mystery; it clouded all things with the dust and ashes of distrust. All disappointment of place, of avarice, of incompetency or ambition, was clearly attributable to it. It even permeated private and social life; there were Rings in our kitchen and household service; in our public schools, that kept the active intelligences of our children passive; there were Rings of engaging, handsome, dissolute young fellows, who kept us moral but unengaging seniors from the favors of the fair; there were subtle, conspiring Rings among our creditors, which sent us into bankruptcy and restricted our credit. In fact it would not be hazardous to say that all that was calamitous in public and private experience was clearly traceable to that combination of power in a minority over weakness in a majority—known as a Ring.

Haply there was a body of demigods, as yet uninvoked, who should speedily settle all that. When Smith of Minnesota, Robinson of Vermont, and Jones of Georgia returned to Congress from these rural seclusions so potent with information and so freed from local prejudices, it was understood, vaguely, that great things would be done. This was always understood. There never was a time in the history of American politics when, to use the expression of the journals before alluded to, "the present session of Congress" did not "bid fair to be the most momentous in our history," and did not, as far as the facts go, leave a vast amount of unfinished important business lying hopelessly upon its desks, having "bolted" the rest as rashly and with as little regard to digestion or assimilation as the American traveller has for his railway refreshment.

In this capital, on this languid midsummer day, in an upper room of one of its second-rate hotels, the Honorable Pratt C. Gashwiler sat at his writing-table. There are certain large, fleshy men with whom the omission of even a necktie or collar has all the effect of an indecent exposure. The Hon. Mr. Gashwiler, in his trousers and shirt, was a sight to be avoided by the modest eye. There were such palpable suggestions of vast extents of unctuous flesh in the slight glimpse offered by his open throat that his dishabille should have been as private as his business. Nevertheless, when there was a knock at his door he unhesitatingly said, "Come in!"—pushing away a goblet crowned with a certain aromatic herb with his right hand, while he drew towards him with his left a few proof slips of his forthcoming speech.

The Gashwiler brow became, as it were, intelligently abstracted.

The intruder regarded Gashwiler with a glance of familiar recognition from his right eye, while his left took in a rapid survey of the papers on the table, and gleamed sardonically.

"You are at work, I see," he said apologetically.

"Yes," replied the Congressman, with an air of perfunctory weariness,—"one of my speeches. Those d—d printers make such a mess of it; I suppose I don't write a very fine hand."

If the gifted Gashwiler had added that he did not write a very intelligent hand, or a very grammatical hand, and that his spelling was faulty, he would have been truthful, although the copy and proof before him might not have borne him out. The near fact was that the speech was composed and written by one Expectant Dobbs, a poor retainer of Gashwiler, and the honorable member's labor as a proof-reader was confined to the introduction of such words as "anarchy," "oligarchy," "satrap," "palladium," and "Argus-eyed" in the proof, with little relevancy as to position or place, and no perceptible effect as to argument.

The stranger saw all this with his wicked left eye, but continued to beam mildly with his right. Removing the coat and waistcoat of Gashwiler from a chair, he drew it towards the table, pushing aside a portly, loud-ticking watch,—the very image of Gashwiler,—that lay beside him, and, resting his elbows on the proofs, said:

"Well?"

"Have you anything new?" asked the parliamentary Gashwiler.

"Much! a woman!" replied the stranger.

The astute Gashwiler, waiting further information, concluded to receive this fact gaily and gallantly. "A woman?—my dear Mr. Wiles,—of course! The dear creatures," he continued, with a fat, offensive chuckle, "somehow are always making their charming presence felt. Ha! ha! A man, sir, in public life becomes accustomed to that sort of thing, and knows when he must be agreeable,—agreeable, sir, but firm! I've had my experience, sir,—my OWN experience,"—and the Congressman leaned back in his chair, not unlike a robust St. Anthony who had withstood one temptation to thrive on another.

"Yes," said Wiles impatiently, "but d—n it, she's on the OTHER SIDE."

"The other side!" repeated Gashwiler vacantly.

"Yes, she's a niece of Garcia's. A little she devil."

"But Garcia's on our side," rejoined Gashwiler.

"Yes, but she is bought by the Ring."

"A woman!" sneered Mr. Gashwiler; "what can she do with men who won't be made fools of? Is she so handsome?"

"I never saw any great beauty in her," said Wiles shortly, "although they say that she's rather caught that d—d Thatcher, in spite of his coldness. At any rate, she is his protegee. But she isn't the sort you're thinking of, Gashwiler. They say she knows, or pretends to know, something about the grant. She may have got hold of some of her uncle's papers. Those Greasers were always d—d fools; and, if he did anything foolish, like as not he bungled or didn't cover up his tracks. And with his knowledge and facilities too! Why, if I'd—" but here Mr. Wiles stopped to sigh over the inequalities of fortune that wasted opportunities on the less skillful scamp.

Mr. Gashwiler became dignified. "She can do nothing with us," he said potentially.

Wiles turned his wicked eye on him. "Manuel and Miguel, who sold out to our man, are afraid of her. They were our witnesses. I verily believe they'd take back everything if she got after them. And as for Pedro, he thinks she holds the power of life and death over him."

"Pedro! life and death,—what's all this?" said the astonished Gashwiler.

Wiles saw his blunder, but saw also that he had gone too far to stop. "Pedro," he said, "was strongly suspected of having murdered Concho, one of the original locators."

Mr. Gashwiler turned white as a sheet, and then flushed again into an apoplectic glow. "Do you dare to say," he began as soon as he could find his tongue and his legs, for in the exercise of his congressional functions these extreme members supported each other,—"do you mean to say," he stammered in rising rage, "that you have dared to deceive an American lawgiver into legislating upon a measure connected with a capital offense? Do I understand you to say, sir, that murder stands upon the record—stands upon the record, sir,—of this cause to which, as a representative of Remus, I have lent my official aid? Do you mean to say that you have deceived my constituency, whose sacred trust I hold, in inveigling me to hiding a crime from the Argus eyes of justice?" And Mr. Gashwiler looked towards the bell-pull as if about to summon a servant to witness this outrage against the established judiciary.

"The murder, if it WAS a murder, took place before Garcia entered upon this claim, or had a footing in this court," returned Wiles blandly, "and is no part of the record."

"You are sure it is not spread upon the record?"

"I am. You can judge for yourself."

Mr. Gashwiler walked to the window, returned to the table, finished his liquor in a single gulp, and then, with a slight resumption of dignity, said:

"That alters the case."

Wiles glanced with his left eye at the Congressman. The right placidly looked out of the window. Presently he said quietly, "I've brought you the certificates of stock; do you wish them made out in your own name?"

Mr. Gashwiler tried hard to look as if he were trying to recall the meaning of Wiles's words. "Oh!—ah!—umph!—let me see,—oh, yes, the certificates,—certainly! Of course you will make them out in the name of my secretary, Mr. Expectant Dobbs. They will perhaps repay him for the extra clerical labor required in the prosecution of your claim. He is a worthy young man. Although not a public officer, yet he is so near to me that perhaps I am wrong in permitting him to accept a fee for private interests. An American representative cannot be too cautious, Mr. Wiles. Perhaps you had better have also a blank transfer. The stock is, I understand, yet in the future. Mr. Dobbs, though talented and praiseworthy, is poor; he may wish to realize. If some—ahem! some FRIEND—better circumstanced should choose to advance the cash to him and run the risk,—why, it would only be an act of kindness."

"You are proverbially generous, Mr. Gashwiler," said Wiles, opening and shutting his left eye like a dark lantern on the benevolent representative.

"Youth, when faithful and painstaking, should be encouraged," replied Mr. Gashwiler. "I lately had occasion to point this out in a few remarks I had to make before the Sabbath school reunion at Remus. Thank you, I will see that they are—ahem!—conveyed to him. I shall give them to him with my own hand," he concluded, falling back in his chair, as if the better to contemplate the perspective of his own generosity and condescension. Mr. Wiles took his hat and turned to go. Before he reached the door Mr. Gashwiler returned to the social level with a chuckle:

"You say this woman, this Garcia's niece, is handsome and smart?"

"Yes."

"I can set another woman on the track that'll euchre her every time!"

Mr. Wiles was too clever to appear to notice the sudden lapse in the Congressman's dignity, and only said, with his right eye:

"Can you?"

"By G-d, I WILL, or I don't know how to represent Remus."

Mr. Wiles thanked him with his right eye, and looked a dagger with his left. "Good," he said, and added persuasively: "Does she live here?"

The Congressman nodded assent. "An awfully handsome woman,—a particular friend of mine!" Mr. Gashwiler here looked as if he would not mind to have been rallied a little over his intimacy with the fair one; but the astute Mr. Wiles was at the same moment making up his mind, after interpreting the Congressman's look and manner, that he must know this fair incognita if he wished to sway Gashwiler. He determined to bide his time, and withdrew.

The door was scarcely closed upon him when another knock diverted Mr. Gashwiler's attention from his proofs. The door opened to a young man with sandy hair and anxious face. He entered the room deprecatingly, as if conscious of the presence of a powerful being, to be supplicated and feared. Mr. Gashwiler did not attempt to disabuse his mind. "Busy, you see," he said shortly, "correcting your work!"

"I hope it is acceptable?" said the young man timidly.

"Well—yes—it will do," said Gashwiler; "indeed I may say it is satisfactory on the whole," he added with the appearance of a large generosity; "quite satisfactory."

"You have no news, I suppose," continued the young man, with a slight flush, born of pride or expectation.

"No, nothing as yet." Mr. Gashwiler paused as if a thought had struck him.

"I have thought," he said, finally, "that some position—such as a secretaryship with me—would help you to a better appointment. Now, supposing that I make you my private secretary, giving you some important and confidential business. Eh?"

Dobbs looked at his patron with a certain wistful, dog-like

expectancy, moved himself excitedly on his chair seat in a peculiar canine-like anticipation of gratitude, strongly suggesting that he would have wagged his tail if he had one. At which Mr. Gashwiler became more impressive.

"Indeed, I may say I anticipated it by certain papers I have put in your charge and in your name, only taking from you a transfer that might enable me to satisfy my conscience hereafter in recommending you as my—ahem!—private secretary. Perhaps, as a mere form, you might now, while you are here, put your name to these transfers, and, so to speak, begin your duties at once."

The glow of pride and hope that mantled the cheek of poor Dobbs might have melted a harder heart than Gashwiler's. But the senatorial toga had invested Mr. Gashwiler with a more than Roman stoicism towards the feelings of others, and he only fell back in his chair in the pose of conscious rectitude as Dobbs hurriedly signed the paper.

"I shall place them in my portman-tell," said Gashwiler, suiting the word to the action, "for safe keeping. I need not inform you, who are now, as it were, on the threshold of official life, that perfect and inviolable secrecy in all affairs of State"—Mr. G. here motioned toward his portmanteau as if it contained a treaty at least—"is most essential and necessary."

Dobbs assented. "Then my duties will keep me with you here?" he asked doubtfully.

"No, no," said Gashwiler hastily; then, correcting himself, he added: "that is—for the present—no!"

Poor Dobbs's face fell. The near fact was that he had lately had notice to quit his present lodgings in consequence of arrears in his rent, and he had a hopeful reliance that his confidential occupation would carry bread and lodging with it. But he only asked if there were any new papers to make out.

"Ahem! not at present; the fact is I am obliged to give so much of my time to callers—I have to-day been obliged to see half a dozen—that I must lock myself up and say 'Not at home' for the rest of the day." Feeling that this was an intimation that the interview was over, the new private secretary, a little dashed as to his near hopes, but still sanguine of the future, humbly took his leave.

But here a certain Providence, perhaps mindful of poor Dobbs, threw into his simple hands—to be used or not, if he were worthy or capable of using it—a certain power and advantage. He had descended the staircase, and was passing through the lower corridor, when he was made the unwilling witness of a remarkable assault.

It appeared that Mr. Wiles, who had quitted Gashwiler's presence as Dobbs was announced, had other business in the hotel, and in pursuance of it had knocked at room No. 90. In response to the gruff voice that bade him enter, Mr. Wiles opened the door, and espied the figure of a tall, muscular, fiery-bearded man extended on the bed, with the bedclothes carefully tucked under his chin, and his arms lying flat by his side.

Mr. Wiles beamed with his right cheek, and advanced to the bed as if to take the hand of the stranger, who, however, neither by word or sign responded to his salutation.

"Perhaps I'm intruding?" said Mr. Wiles blandly.

"Perhaps you are," said Red Beard dryly.

Mr. Wiles forced a smile on his right cheek, which he turned to the smiter, but permitted the left to indulge in unlimited malevolence. "I wanted merely to know if you have looked into that matter?" he said meekly.

"I've looked into it and round it and across it and over it and through it," responded the man gravely, with his eyes fixed on Wiles.

"And you have perused all the papers?" continued Mr. Wiles.

"I've read every paper, every speech, every affidavit, every decision, every argument," said the stranger as if repeating a formula.

Mr. Wiles attempted to conceal his embarrassment by an easy, right-handed smile, that went off sardonically on the left, and continued: "Then I hope, my dear sir, that, having thoroughly mastered the case, you are inclined to be favorable to us?"

The gentleman in the bed did not reply, but apparently nestled more closely beneath the coverlids.

"I have brought the shares I spoke of," continued Mr. Wiles, insinuatingly.

"Hev you a friend within call?" interrupted the recumbent man gently.

"I don't quite understand!" smiled Mr. Wiles. "Of course any name you might suggest—"

"Hev you a friend, any chap that you might waltz in here at a moment's call?" continued the man in bed. "No? Do you know any of them waiters in the house? Thar's a bell over yan!" and he motioned with his eyes towards the wall, but did not otherwise move his body.

"No," said Wiles, becoming slightly suspicious and wrathful.

"Mebbe a stranger might do? I reckon thar's one passin' in the hall. Call him in,—he'll do!"

Wiles opened the door a little impatiently, yet inquisitively, as Dobbs passed. The man in bed called out, "Oh, stranger!" and, as Dobbs stopped, said, "Come yar."

Dobbs entered a little timidly, as was his habit with strangers.

"I don't know who you be—nor care, I reckon," said the stranger. "This yer man"—pointing to Wiles—"is Wiles. I'm Josh Sibblee of Fresno, Member of Congress from the 4th Congressional District of Californy. I'm jist lying here, with a derringer into each hand,—jist lying here kivered up and holdin' in on'y to keep from blowin' the top o' this d—d skunk's head off. I kinder feel I can't hold in any longer. What I want to say to ye, stranger, is that this yer skunk— which his name is Wiles—hez bin tryin' his d—dest to get a bribe onto Josh, and Josh, outo respect for his constituents, is jist waitin' for some stranger to waltz in and stop the d—dest fight—"

"But, my dear Mr. Sibblee, there must be some mistake," said Wiles earnestly.

"Mistake? Strip me!"

"No! No!" said Wiles, hurriedly, as the simple-minded Dobbs was about to draw down the coverlid.

"Take him away," said the Hon. Mr. Sibblee, "before I disgrace my constituency. They said I'd be in jail afore I get through the session. Ef you've got any humanity, stranger, snake him out, and pow'ful quick, too."

Dobbs, quite white and aghast, looked at Wiles and hesitated. There was a slight movement in the bed. Both men started for the door; and the next minute it closed very decidedly on the member from Fresno.

CHAPTER XI

HOW IT WAS LOBBIED FOR

The Hon. Pratt C. Gashwiler, M.C., was of course unaware
of the incident described in the last chapter. His secret, even
if it had been discovered by Dobbs, was safe in that gentleman's innocent and honorable hands, and certainly was not
of a quality that Mr. Wiles, at present, would have cared to
expose. For, in spite of Mr. Wiles's discomfiture, he still had
enough experience of character to know that the irate member from Fresno would be satisfied with his own peculiar
manner of vindicating his own personal integrity, and would
not make a public scandal of it. Again, Wiles was convinced
that Dobbs was equally implicated with Gashwiler, and
would be silent for his own sake. So that poor Dobbs, as is
too often the fate of simple but weak natures, had full credit
for duplicity by every rascal in the land.

From which it may be inferred that nothing occurred to
disturb the security of Gashwiler. When the door closed
upon Mr. Wiles, he indited a note which, with a costly but
exceedingly distasteful bouquet,—rearranged by his own fat
fingers, and discord and incongruity visible in every combination of color,—he sent off by a special messenger. Then he
proceeded to make his toilet,—an operation rarely graceful
or picturesque in our sex, and an insult to the spectator when

obesity is superadded. When he had put on a clean shirt, of which there was grossly too much, and added a white waistcoat, that seemed to accent his rotundity, he completed his attire with a black frock coat of the latest style, and surveyed himself complacently before a mirror. It is to be recorded that, however satisfactory the result might have been to Mr. Gashwiler, it was not so to the disinterested spectator. There are some men on whom "that deformed thief, Fashion," avenges himself by making their clothes appear perennially new. The gloss of the tailor's iron never disappears; the creases of the shelf perpetually rise in judgment against the wearer. Novelty was the general suggestion of Mr. Gashwiler's full-dress,—it was never his HABITUDE;—and "Our own Make," "Nobby," and the "Latest Style, only $15," was as patent on the legislator's broad back as if it still retained the shop-man's ticket.

Thus arrayed, within an hour he complacently followed the note and his floral offering. The house he sought had been once the residence of a foreign Ambassador, who had loyally represented his government in a single unimportant treaty, now forgotten, and in various receptions and dinners, still actively remembered by occasional visits to its salon; now the average dreary American parlor. "Dear me," the fascinating Mr. X would say, "but do you know, love, in this very room I remember meeting the distinguished Marquis of Monte Pio;" or perhaps the fashionable Jones of the State Department instantly crushed the decayed friend he was perfunctorily visiting by saying, "'Pon my soul, YOU here;— why, the last time I was in this room I gossiped for an hour with the Countess de Castenet in that very corner." For, with the recall of the aforesaid Ambassador, the mansion had become a boarding-place, kept by the wife of a departmental clerk.

Perhaps there was nothing in the history of the house more

quaint and philosophic than the story of its present occupant. Roger Fauquier had been a departmental clerk for forty years. It was at once his practical good luck and his misfortune to have been early appointed to a position which required a thorough and complete knowledge of the formulas and routine of a department that expended millions of the public funds. Fauquier, on a poor salary, diminishing instead of increasing with his service, had seen successive administrations bud and blossom and decay, but had kept his position through the fact that his knowledge was a necessity to the successive chiefs and employes. Once it was true that he had been summarily removed by a new Secretary, to make room for a camp follower, whose exhaustive and intellectual services in a political campaign had made him eminently fit for anything; but the alarming discovery that the new clerk's knowledge of grammar and etymology was even worse than that of the Secretary himself, and that, through ignorance of detail, the business of that department was retarded to a damage to the Government of over half a million of dollars, led to the reinstatement of Mr. Fauquier— AT A LOWER SALARY. For it was felt that something was wrong somewhere, and as it had always been the custom of Congress and the administration to cut down salaries as the first step to reform, they made of Mr. Fauquier a moral example. A gentleman born, of somewhat expensive tastes, having lived up to his former salary, this change brought another bread-winner into the field, Mrs. Fauquier, who tried, more or less unsuccessfully, to turn her old Southern habits of hospitality to remunerative account. But as poor Fauquier could never be prevailed upon to present a bill to a gentleman, sir, and as some of the scions of the best Southern families were still waiting for, or had been recently dismissed from, a position, the experiment was a pecuniary failure. Yet the house was of excellent repute and well patronized; indeed, it was worth something to see old Fauquier sitting at the head of his own table, in something of his ancestral style, relating anecdotes of great men now dead and gone, interrupted only by occasional visits from importunate tradesmen.

Prominent among what Mr. Fauquier called his "little family" was a black-eyed lady of great powers of fascination, and considerable local reputation as a flirt. Nevertheless, these social aberrations were amply condoned by a facile and complacent husband, who looked with a lenient and even admiring eye upon the little lady's amusement, and to a certain extent lent a tacit indorsement to her conduct. Nobody minded Hopkinson; in the blaze of Mrs. Hopkinson's fascinations he was completely lost sight of. A few married women with unduly sensitive husbands, and several single ladies of the best and longest standing, reflected severely on her conduct. The younger men of course admired her, but I think she got her chief support from old fogies like ourselves. For it is your quiet, self-conceited, complacent, philosophic, broad-waisted pater-familias who, after all, is the one to whom the gay and giddy of the proverbially impulsive, unselfish sex owe their place in the social firmament. We are never inclined to be captious; we laugh at as a folly what our wives and daughters condemn as a fault; OUR "withers are unwrung," yet we still confess to the fascinations of a pretty face. We know, bless us, from dear experience, the exact value of one woman's opinion of another; we want our brilliant little friend to shine; it is only the moths who will burn their two-penny immature wings in the flame! And why should they not? Nature has been pleased to supply more moths than candles! Go to!—give the pretty creature—be she maid, wife, or widow—a show! And so, my dear sir, while mater-familias bends her black brows in disgust, we smile our superior little smile, and extend to Mistress Anonyma our gracious indorsement. And if giddiness is grateful, or if folly is friendly,—well, of course, we can't help that. Indeed it rather proves our theory.

I had intended to say something about Hopkinson; but really there is very little to say. He was invariably good humored. A few ladies once tried to show him that he really ought to feel worse than he did about the conduct of his wife; and it is recorded that Hopkinson, in an excess of good humor and kindliness, promised to do so. Indeed the good fellow was so accessible that it is said that young DeLancy of the Tape Department confided to Hopkinson his jealousy of a rival; and revealed the awful secret that he (DeLancy) had reason to expect more loyalty from his (Hopkinson's) wife. The good fellow is reported to have been very sympathetic, and to have promised Delaney to lend whatever influence he had with Mrs. Hopkinson in his favor. "You see," he said explanatorily to DeLancy, "she has a good deal to attend to lately, and I suppose has got rather careless,—that's women's ways. But if I can't bring her round I'll speak to Gashwiler,—I'll get him to use his influence with Mrs. Hop. So cheer up, my boy, HE'LL make it all right."

The appearance of a bouquet on the table of Mrs. Hopkinson was no rare event; nevertheless, Mr. Gashwiler's was not there. Its hideous contrasts had offended her woman's eye,—it is observable that good taste survives the wreck of all the other feminine virtues,—and she had distributed it to make boutonnieres for other gentlemen. Yet, when he appeared, she said to him hastily, putting her little hand over the cardiac region:

"I'm so glad you came. But you gave me SUCH a fright an hour ago."

Mr. Gashwiler was both pleased and astounded. "What have I done, my dear Mrs. Hopkinson?" he began.

"Oh, don't talk," she said sadly. "What have you done, indeed! Why, you sent me that beautiful bouquet. I could not mistake your taste in the arrangement of the flowers;—but my husband was here. You know his jealousy. I was obliged to conceal it from him. Never—promise me now—NEVER do it again."

Mr. Gashwiler gallantly protested.

"No! I am serious! I was so agitated: he must have seen me blush."

Nothing but the gross flattery to this speech could have clouded its manifest absurdity to the Gashwiler consciousness. But Mr. Gashwiler had already succumbed to the girlish half-timidity with which it was uttered. Nevertheless, he could not help saying:

"But why should he be so jealous now? Only day before yesterday I saw Simpson of Duluth hand you a nosegay right before him!"

"Ah," returned the lady, "he was outwardly calm THEN, but you know nothing of the scene that occurred between us after you left."

"But," gasped the practical Gashwiler, "Simpson had given your husband that contract,—a cool fifty thousand in his pocket!"

Mrs. Hopkinson looked as dignifiedly at Gashwiler as was consistent with five feet three (the extra three inches being a pyramidal structure of straw-colored hair), a frond of faint curls, a pair of laughing blue eyes, and a small belted waist. Then she said, with a casting down of her lids:

"You forget that my husband loves me." And for once the minx appeared to look penitent. It was becoming; but as it had been originally practiced in a simple white dress, relieved only with pale-blue ribbons, it was not entirely in keeping with be-flounced lavender and rose-colored trimmings. Yet the woman who hesitates between her moral expression and the harmony of her dress is lost. And Mrs. Hopkinson was victrix by her very audacity.

Mr. Gashwiler was flattered. The most dissolute man likes the appearance of virtue. "But graces and accomplishments like yours, dear Mrs. Hopkinson," he said oleaginously, "belong to the whole country." Which, with something between a courtesy and a strut, he endeavored to represent. "And I shall want to avail myself of all," he added, "in the matter of the Castro claim. A little supper at Welcker's, a glass or two of champagne, and a single flash of those bright eyes, and the thing is done."

"But," said Mrs. Hopkinson, "I've promised Josiah that I would give up all those frivolities, and although my conscience is clear, you know how people talk! Josiah hears it. Why, only last night, at a reception at the Patagonian Minister's, every woman in the room gossiped about me because I led the german with him. As if a married woman, whose husband was interested in the Government, could not be civil to the representative of a friendly power?"

Mr. Gashwiler did not see how Mr. Hopkinson's late contract for supplying salt pork and canned provisions to the army of the United States should make his wife susceptible to the advances of foreign princes; but he prudently kept that to himself. Still, not being himself a diplomat, he could not help saying:

"But I understood that Mr. Hopkinson did not object to your

interesting yourself in this claim, and you know some of the stock—"

The lady started, and said:

"Stock! Dear Mr. Gashwiler, for Heaven's sake don't mention that hideous name to me. Stock, I am sick of it! Have you gentlemen no other topic for a lady?"

She punctuated her sentence with a mischievous look at her interlocutor. For a second time I regret to say that Mr. Gashwiler succumbed. The Roman constituency at Remus, it is to be hoped, were happily ignorant of this last defection of their great legislator. Mr. Gashwiler instantly forgot his theme,—began to ply the lady with a certain bovine-like gallantry, which it is to be said to her credit she parried with a playful, terrier-like dexterity, when the servant suddenly announced, "Mr. Wiles."

Gashwiler started. Not so Mrs. Hopkinson, who, however, prudently and quietly removed her own chair several inches from Gashwiler's.

"Do you know Mr. Wiles?" she asked pleasantly.

"No! That is, I—ah—yes, I may say I have had some business relations with him," responded Gashwiler rising.

"Won't you stay?" she added pleadingly. "Do!"

Mr. Gashwiler's prudence always got the better of his gallantry. "Not now," he responded in some nervousness. "Perhaps I had better go now, in view of what you have just said about gossip. You need not mention my name to this-er—this—Mr. Wiles." And with one eye on the door, and an awkward dash of his lips at the lady's fingers, he withdrew.

There was no introductory formula to Mr. Wiles's interview. He dashed at once in medias res. "Gashwiler knows a woman that, he says, can help us against that Spanish girl who is coming here with proofs, prettiness, fascination, and what not! You must find her out."

"Why?" asked the lady laughingly.

"Because I don't trust that Gashwiler. A woman with a pretty face and an ounce of brains could sell him out; aye, and US with him."

"Oh, say TWO ounces of brains. Mr. Wiles, Mr. Gashwiler is no fool."

"Possibly, except when your sex is concerned, and it is very likely that the woman is his superior."

"I should think so," said Mrs. Hopkinson with a mischievous look.

"Ah, you know her, then?"

"Not so well as I know him," said Mrs. H. quite seriously. "I wish I did."

"Well, you'll find out if she's to be trusted! You are laughing,—it is a serious matter! This woman—"

Mrs. Hopkinson dropped him a charming courtesy and said,

"C'est moi!"

CHAPTER XII

A RACE FOR IT

Royal Thatcher worked hard. That the boyish little painter who shared his hospitality at the "Blue Mass" mine should afterward have little part in his active life seemed not inconsistent with his habits. At present the mine was his only mistress, claiming his entire time, exasperating him with fickleness, but still requiring that supreme devotion of which his nature was capable. It is possible that Miss Carmen saw this too, and so set about with feminine tact, if not to supplement, at least to make her rival less pertinacious and absorbing. Apart from this object, she zealously labored in her profession, yet with small pecuniary result, I fear. Local art was at a discount in California. The scenery of the country had not yet become famous; rather it was reserved for a certain Eastern artist, already famous, to make it so; and people cared little for the reproduction, under their very noses, of that which they saw continually with their own eyes, and valued not. So that little Mistress Carmen was fain to divert her artist soul to support her plump little material body; and made divers excursions into the regions of ceramic art, painting on velvet, illuminating missals, decorating china, and the like. I have in my possession some wax flowers—a startling fuchsia and a bewildering dahlia—sold for a mere pittance by this little lady, whose pictures lately took the prize at a foreign exhibition, shortly after she had been half starved by a California public, and claimed by a California press as its fostered child of genius.

Of these struggles and triumphs Thatcher had no knowledge; yet he was perhaps more startled than he would own to himself when, one December day, he received this despatch: "Come to Washington at once.—Carmen de Haro."

"Carmen de Haro!" I grieve to state that such was the preoccupation of this man, elected by fate to be the hero of the solitary amatory episode of his story, that for a moment he could not recall her. When the honest little figure that had so manfully stood up against him, and had proved her sex by afterwards running away from him, came back at last to his memory, he was at first mystified and then self-reproachful. He had been, he felt vaguely, untrue to himself. He had been remiss to the self-confessed daughter of his enemy. Yet why should she telegraph to him, and what was she doing in Washington? To all these speculations it is to be said to his credit that he looked for no sentimental or romantic answer. Royal Thatcher was naturally modest and self-depreciating in his relations to the other sex, as indeed most men who are apt to be successful with women generally are, despite a vast degree of superannuated bosh to the contrary. To the half dozen women who are startled by sheer audacity into submission there are scores who are piqued by a self-respectful patience; and where a women has to do half the wooing, she generally makes a pretty sure thing of it.

In his bewilderment Thatcher had overlooked a letter lying on his table. It was from his Washington lawyer. The concluding paragraph caught his eye,—"Perhaps it would be well if you came here yourself. Roscommon is here; and they say there is a niece of Garcia's, lately appeared, who is likely to get up a strong social sympathy for the old Mexican. I don't know that they expect to prove anything by her; but I'm told she is attractive and clever, and has enlisted the sympathies of the delegation." Thatcher laid the letter down a little indignantly. Strong men are quite as liable as weak women are to sudden inconsistencies on any question they may have in common. What right had this poor little bud he had cherished,—he was quite satisfied now that he had cherished her, and really had suffered from her absence,— what right had she to suddenly blossom in the sunshine of power to be, perhaps, plucked and worn by one of his enemies? He did not agree with his lawyer that she was in any way connected with his enemies: he trusted to her masculine loyalty that far. But here was something vaguely dangerous to the feminine mind,—position, flattery, power. He was almost as firmly satisfied now that he had been wronged and neglected as he had been positive a few moments before that he had been remiss in his attention. The irritation, although momentary, was enough to decide this strong man. He telegraphed to San Francisco; and, having missed the steamer, secured an overland passage to Washington; thought better of it, and partly changed his mind an hour after the ticket was purchased; but, manlike, having once made a practical step in a wrong direction, he kept on rather than admit an inconsistency to himself. Yet he was not entirely satisfied that his journey was a business one. The impulsive, weak little Mistress Carmen had prudently scored one against the strong man.

Only a small part of the present great trans-continental railway at this time had been built, and was but piers at either end of a desolate and wild expanse as yet unbridged. When the overland traveller left the rail at Reno, he left, as it were, civilization with it; and, until he reached the Nebraska frontier, the rest of his road was only the old emigrant trail traversed by the coaches of the Overland Company. Excepting a part of "Devil's Canyon," the way was unpicturesque and flat; and the passage of the Rocky Mountains, far from suggesting the alleged poetry of that region, was only a reminder of those sterile distances of a level New England landscape.

The journey was a dreary monotony that was scarcely enlivened by its discomforts, never amounting to actual accident or incident, but utterly destructive to all nervous tissue. Insanity often supervened. "On the third day out," said Hank Monk, driver, speaking casually but charitably of a "fare,"—"on the third day out, after axing no end of questions and getting no answers, he took to chewing straws that he picked outer the cushion, and kussin' to hisself. From that very day I knew it was all over with him, and I handed him over to his friends at 'Shy Ann,' strapped to the back seat, and ravin' and cussin' at Ben Holliday, the gent'manly proprietor." It is presumed that the unfortunate tourist's indignation was excited at the late Mr. Benjamin Holliday, then the proprietor of the line,—an evidence of his insanity that no one who knew that large-hearted, fastidious, and elegantly-cultured Californian, since allied to foreign nobility, will for a moment doubt.

Mr. Royal Thatcher was too old and experienced a mountaineer to do aught but accept patiently and cynically his brother Californian's method of increasing his profits. As it was generally understood that any one who came from California by that route had some dark design, the victim received little sympathy. Thatcher's equable temperament and indomitable will stood him in good stead, and helped him cheerfully in this emergency. He ate his scant meals, and otherwise took care of the functions of his weak human nature, when and where he could, without grumbling, and at times earned even the praise of his driver by his ability to "rough it." Which "roughing it," by the way, meant the ability of the passengers to accept the incompetency of the

Company. It is true there were times when he regretted that he had not taken the steamer; but then he reflected that he was one of a Vigilance Committee, sworn to hang that admirable man, the late Commodore Cornelius Vanderbilt, for certain practices and cruelties done upon the bodies of certain steerage passengers by his line, and for divers irregularities in their transportation. I mention this fact merely to show how so practical and stout a voyager as Thatcher might have confounded the perplexities attending the administration of a great steamship company with selfish greed and brutality; and that he, with other Californians, may not have known the fact, since recorded by the Commodore's family clergyman, that the great millionaire was always true to the hymns of his childhood.

Nevertheless, Thatcher found time to be cheerful and helpful to his fellow passengers, and even to be so far interesting to "Yuba Bill," the driver, as to have the box seat placed at his disposal. "But," said Thatcher, in some concern, "the box seat was purchased by that other gentleman in Sacramento. He paid extra for it, and his name's on your way-bill!" "That," said Yuba Bill, scornfully, "don't fetch me even ef he'd chartered the whole shebang. Look yar, do you reckon I'm goin' to spile my temper by setting next to a man with a game eye? And such an eye! Gewhillikins! Why, darn my skin, the other day when we war watering at Webster's, he got down and passed in front of the off-leader,—that yer pinto colt that's bin accustomed to injins, grizzlies, and buffalo, and I'm bless ef, when her eye tackled his, ef she didn't jist git up and rar round that I reckoned I'd hev to go down and take them blinders off from HER eyes and clap on HIS." "But he paid the money, and is entitled to his seat," persisted Thatcher. "Mebbe he is—in the office of the Kempeny," growled Yuba Bill; "but it's time some folks knowed that out in the plains I run this yer team myself."—A fact which was self-evident to most of the passengers. "I suppose his authority is as absolute on this dreary waste as a ship captain's in mid ocean," exclaimed Thatcher to the baleful-eyed stranger. Mr. Wiles—whom the reader has recognized—assented with the public side of his face, but looked vengeance at Yuba Bill with the other, while Thatcher, innocent of the presence of one of his worst enemies, placated Bill so far as to restore Wiles to his rights. Wiles thanked him. "Shall I have the pleasure of your company far?" Wiles asked insinuatingly. "To Washington," replied Thatcher frankly. "Washington is a gay city during the session," again suggested the stranger. "I'm going on business," said Thatcher bluntly.

A trifling incident occurred at Pine-Tree Crossing which did not heighten Yuba Bill's admiration of the stranger. As Bill opened the double-locked box in the "boot" of the coach—sacred to Wells, Fargo & Co.'s Express and the Overland Company's treasures—Mr. Wiles perceived a small, black morocco portemanteau among the parcels. "Ah, you carry baggage there too?" he said sweetly. "Not often," responded Yuba Bill shortly. "Ah, this then contains valuables?" "It belongs to that man whose seat you've got," said Yuba Bill, who, for insulting purposes of his own, preferred to establish the fiction that Wiles was an interloper; "and ef he reckons, in a sorter mixed kempeny like this, to lock up his portmantle, I don't know who's business it is. Who?" continued Bill, lashing himself into a simulated rage, "who, in blank, is running this yer team? Hey? Mebbe you think, sittin' up thar on the box seat, you are. Mebbe you think you kin see round corners with that thar eye, and kin pull up for teams round corners, on down grades, a mile ahead?" But here Thatcher, who, with something of Lancelot's concern for Modred, had a noble pity for all infirmities, interfered so sternly that Yuba Bill stopped.

On the fourth day they struck a blinding snow-storm, while

ascending the dreary plateau that henceforward for six hundred miles was to be their roadbed. The horses, after floundering through the drift, gave out completely on reaching the next station, and the prospects ahead, to all but the experienced eye, looked doubtful. A few passengers advised taking to sledges, others a postponement of the journey until the weather changed. Yuba Bill alone was for pressing forward as they were. "Two miles more and we're on the high grade, whar the wind is strong enough to blow you through the windy, and jist peart enough to pack away over them cliffs every inch of snow that falls. I'll jist skirmish round in and out o' them drifts on these four wheels whar ye can't drag one o' them flat-bottomed dry-goods boxes through a drift." Bill had a California whip's contempt for a sledge. But he was warmly seconded by Thatcher, who had the next best thing to experience, the instinct that taught him to read character, and take advantage of another man's experience. "Them that wants to stop kin do so," said Bill authoritatively, cutting the Gordian knot; "them as wants to take a sledge can do so,—thar's one in the barn. Them as wants to go on with me and the relay will come on." Mr. Wiles selected the sledge and a driver, a few remained for the next stage, and Thatcher, with two others, decided to accompany Yuba Bill. These changes took up some valuable time; and the storm continuing, the stage was run under the shed, the passengers gathering around the station fire; and not until after midnight did Yuba Bill put in the relays. "I wish you a good journey," said Wiles, as he drove from the shed as Bill entered. Bill vouchsafed no reply, but, addressing himself to the driver, said curtly, as if giving an order for the delivery of goods, "Shove him out at Rawlings," and passed contemptuously around to the tail board of the sled, and returned to the harnessing of his relay.

The moon came out and shone high as Yuba Bill once more took the reins in his hands. The wind, which instantly attacked them as they reached the level, seemed to make the driver's theory plausible, and for half a mile the roadbed was swept clean, and frozen hard. Further on a tongue of snow, extending from a boulder to the right, reached across their path to the height of two or three feet. But Yuba Bill dashed through a part of it, and by skillful maneuvering circumvented the rest. But even as the obstacle was passed, the coach dropped with an ominous lurch on one side, and the off fore wheel flew off in the darkness. Bill threw the horses back on their haunches; but, before their momentum could be checked, the near hind wheel slipped away, the vehicle rocked violently, plunged backwards and forwards, and stopped.

Yuba Bill was on the road in an instant with his lantern. Then followed an outbreak of profanity which I regret, for artistic purposes, exceeds that generous limit which a sympathizing public has already extended to me in the explication of character. Let me state, therefore, that in a very few moments he succeeded in disparaging the characters of his employers, their male and female relatives, the coach builder, the station keeper, the road on which he travelled, and the travellers themselves, with occasional broad expletives addressed to himself and his own relatives. For the spirit of this and a more cultivated poetry of expression, I beg to refer the temperate reader to the 3d chapter of Job.

The passengers knew Bill, and sat, conservative, patient, and expectant. As yet the cause of the catastrophe was not known. At last Thatcher's voice came from the box seat:

"What's up, Bill?"

"Not a blank lynch pin in the whole blank coach," was the answer.

There was a dead silence. Yuba Bill executed a wild war dance of helpless rage.

"Blank the blank ENCHANTED thing to blank!"

(I beg here to refer the fastidious and cultivated reader to the only adjective I have dared transcribe of this actual oath which I once had the honor of hearing. He will I trust not fail to recognize the old classic daemon in this wild western objurgation.)

"Who did it?" asked Thatcher.

Yuba Bill did not reply, but dashed up again to the box, unlocked the "boot," and screamed out:

"The man that stole your portmantle,—Wiles!"

Thatcher laughed:

"Don't worry about that, Bill. A 'biled' shirt, an extra collar, and a few papers. Nothing more."

Yuba Bill slowly descended. When he reached the ground, he plucked Thatcher aside by his coat sleeve:

"Ye don't mean to say ye had nothing in that bag ye was trying to get away with?"

"No," said the laughing Thatcher frankly.

"And that Wiles warn't one o' them detectives?"

"Not to my knowledge, certainly."

Yuba Bill sighed sadly, and returned to assist in the replacing

Bret Harte

of the coach on its wheels again.

"Never mind, Bill," said one of the passengers sympathizingly, "we'll catch that man Wiles at Rawlings sure;" and he looked around at the inchoate vigilance committee, already "rounding into form" about him.

"Ketch him!" returned Yuba Bill, derisively, "why we've got to go back to the station; and afore we're off agin he's pinted fur Clarmont on the relay we lose. Ketch him! H-ll's full of such ketches!"

There was clearly nothing to do but to go back to the station to await the repairing of the coach. While this was being done Yuba Bill again drew Thatcher aside:

"I allers suspected that chap's game eye, but I didn't somehow allow for anything like this. I reckoned it was only the square thing to look arter things gen'rally, and 'specially your traps. So, to purvent troubil, and keep things about ekal, ez he was goin' away, I sorter lifted this yer bag of hiz outer the tail board of his sleigh. I don't know as it is any exchange or compensation, but it may give ye a chance to spot him agin, or him you. It strikes me as bein' far-minded and squar';" and with these words he deposited at the feet of the astounded Thatcher the black travelling bag of Mr. Wiles.

"But, Bill,—see here! I can't take this!" interrupted Thatcher hastily. "You can't swear that he's taken my bag,—and—and, —blank it all,—this won't do, you know. I've no right to this man's things, even if—"

"Hold your hosses," said Bill gravely; "I ondertook to take charge o' your traps. I didn't—at least that d—d wall-eyed— Thar's a portmantle! I don't know who's it is. Take it."

Half amused, half embarrassed, yet still protesting, Thatcher took the bag in his hands.

"Ye might open it in my presence," suggested Yuba Bill gravely.

Thatcher, half laughingly, did so. It was full of papers and semi-legal-looking documents. Thatcher's own name on one of them caught his eye; he opened the paper hastily and perused it. The smile faded from his lips.

"Well," said Yuba Bill, "suppose we call it a fair exchange at present."

Thatcher was still examining the papers. Suddenly this cautious, strong-minded man looked up into Yuba Bill's waiting face, and said quietly, in the despicable slang of the epoch and region:

"It's a go! Suppose we do."

CHAPTER XIII

HOW IT BECAME FAMOUS

Yuba Bill was right in believing that Wiles would lose no time at Rawlings. He left there on a fleet horse before Bill had returned with the broken-down coach to the last station, and distanced the telegram sent to detain him two hours. Leaving the stage road and its dangerous telegraphic stations, he pushed southward to Denver over the army trail, in company with a half-breed packer, crossing the Missouri before Thatcher had reached Julesburg. When Thatcher was at Omaha, Wiles was already in St. Louis; and as the Pullman car containing the hero of the "Blue Mass" mine rolled into Chicago, Wiles was already walking the streets of the national capital. Nevertheless, he had time en route to sink in the waters of the North Platte, with many expressions of disgust, the little black portmanteau belonging to Thatcher, containing his dressing case, a few unimportant letters, and an extra shirt, to wonder why simple men did not travel with their important documents and valuables, and to set on foot some prudent and cautious inquiries regarding his own lost carpet bag and its important contents.

But for these trifles he had every reason to be satisfied with the progress of his plans. "It's all right," said Mrs. Hopkinson merrily; "while you and Gashwiler have been working with your 'stock,' and treating the whole world as if it could be bribed, I've done more with that earnest, self-believing, self-deceiving, and perfectly pathetic Roscommon than all you fellows put together. Why, I've told his pitiful story, and drawn tears from the eyes of Senators and Cabinet Ministers. More than that, I've introduced him into society, put him in a dress coat,—such a figure!—and you know how the best folk worship everything that is outre as the sincere thing. I've made him a complete success. Why, only the other night, when Senator Misnancy and Judge Fitzdawdle were here, after making him tell his story,—which you know I think he really believes,—I sang 'There came to the beach a poor Exile of Erin,' and my husband told me afterwards it was worth at least a dozen votes."

"But about this rival of yours,—this niece of Garcia's?"

"Another of your blunders; you men know nothing of women. Firstly, she's a swarthy little brunette, with dots for eyes; and strides like a man, dresses like a dowdy, don't wear stays, and has no style. Then, she's a single woman, and alone; and, although she affects to be an artist, and has Bohemian ways, don't you see she can't go into society without a chaperon or somebody to go with her? Nonsense."

"But," persisted Wiles, "she must have some power; there's Judge Mason and Senator Peabody, who are constantly talking about her; and Dinwiddie of Virginia escorted her through the Capitol the other day."

Mistress Hopkinson laughed. "Mason and Peabody aspire to be thought literary and artistic, and Dinwiddie wanted to pique ME!"

"But Thatcher is no fool—"

"Is Thatcher a lady's man?" queried the lady suddenly.

"Hardly, I should say," responded Wiles. "He pretends to be absorbed in his swindle and devoted to his mine; and I don't think that even you—" he stopped with a slight sneer.

"There, you are misunderstanding me again, and, what is worse, you are misunderstanding your case. Thatcher is pleased with her because he has probably seen no one else. Wait till he comes to Washington and has an opportunity for comparison;" and she cast a frank glance at her mirror, where Wiles, with a sardonic bow, left her standing.

Mr. Gashwiler was quite as confident of his own success with Congress. "We are within a few days of the end of the session. We will manage to have it taken up and rushed through before that fellow Thatcher knows what he is about."

"If it could be done before he gets here," said Wiles, "it's a reasonably sure thing. He is delayed two days: he might have been delayed longer." Here Mr. Wiles sighed. If the accident had happened on a mountain road, and the stage had been precipitated over the abyss, what valuable time would have been saved, and success become a surety. But Mr. Wiles's functions as an advocate did not include murder; at least, he was doubtful if it could be taxed as costs.

"We need have no fears, sir," resumed Mr. Gashwiler; "The matter is now in the hands of the highest tribunal of appeal in the country. It will meet, sir, with inflexible justice. I have already prepared some remarks—"

"By the way," interrupted Wiles infelicitously, "where's your young man,—your private secretary,—Dobbs?"

The Congressman for a moment looked confused. "He is not

here. And I must correct your error in applying that term to him. I have never put my confidence in the hands of any one."

"But you introduced him to me as your secretary?"

"A mere honorary title, sir. A brevet rank. I might, it is true, have thought to repose such a trust in him. But I was deceived, sir, as I fear I am too apt to be when I permit my feelings as a man to overcome my duty as an American legislator. Mr. Dobbs enjoyed my patronage and the opportunity it gave me to introduce him into public life only to abuse it. He became, I fear, deeply indebted. His extravagance was unlimited, his ambition unbounded, but without, sir, a cash basis. I advanced money to him from time to time upon the little property you so generously extended to him for his services. But it was quickly dissipated. Yet, sir, such is the ingratitude of man that his family lately appealed to me for assistance. I felt it was necessary to be stern, and I refused. I would not for the sake of his family say anything, but I have missed, sir, books from my library. On the day after he left, two volumes of Patent Office reports and a Blue Book of Congress, purchased that day by me at a store on Pennsylvania avenue, were MISSING,—missing! I had difficulty, sir, great difficulty in keeping it from the papers!"

As Mr. Wiles had heard the story already from Gashwiler's acquaintances, with more or less free comment on the gifted legislator's economy, he could not help thinking that the difficulty had been great indeed. But he only fixed his malevolent eye on Gashwiler and said:

"So he is gone, eh?"

"Yes."

"And you've made an enemy of him? That's bad."

Mr. Gashwiler tried to look dignifiedly unconcerned; but something in his visitor's manner made him uneasy.

"I say it is bad, if you have. Listen. Before I left here, I found at a boardinghouse where he had boarded, and still owed a bill, a trunk which the landlord retained. Opening it, I found some letters and papers to yours, with certain memoranda of his, which I thought ought to be in YOUR possession. As an alleged friend of his, I redeemed the trunk by paying the amount of his bill, and secured the more valuable papers."

Gashwiler, whose face had grown apoplectically suffused as Wiles went on, at last gasped: "But you got the trunk, and have the papers?"

"Unfortunately, no; and that's why it's bad."

"But, good God! what have you done with them?"

"I've lost them somewhere on the Overland Road."

Mr. Gashwiler sat for a few moments speechless, vacillating between a purple rage and a pallid fear. Then he said hoarsely:

"They are all blank forgeries,—every one of them."

"Oh, no!" said Wiles, smiling blandly on his dexter side, and enjoying the whole scene malevolently with his sinister eye. "YOUR papers are all genuine, and I won't say are not all right, but unfortunately I had in the same bag some memoranda of my own for the use of my client, that, you understand, might be put to some bad use if found by a clever man."

The two rascals looked at each other. There is on the whole really very little "honor among thieves,"—at least great ones,—and the inferior rascal succumbed at the reflection of what HE might do if he were in the other rascal's place. "See here, Wiles," he said, relaxing his dignity with the perspiration that oozed from every pore, and made the collar of his shirt a mere limp rag. "See here, WE"—this first use of the plural was equivalent to a confession—"we must get them papers."

"Of course," said Wiles coolly, "if we CAN, and if Thatcher doesn't get wind of them."

"He cannot."

"He was on the coach when I lost them, coming East."

Mr. Gashwiler paled again. In the emergency he had recourse to the sideboard and a bottle, forgetting Wiles. Ten minutes before Wiles would have remained seated; but it is recorded that he rose, took the bottle from the gifted Gashwiler's fingers, helped himself FIRST, and then sat down.

"Yes, but, my boy," said Gashwiler, now rapidly changing situations with the cooler Wiles; "yes, but, old fellow," he added, poking Wiles with a fat forefinger, "don't you see the whole thing will be up before he gets here?"

"Yes," said Wiles gloomily, "but those lazy, easy, honest men have a way of popping up just at the nick of time. They never need hurry; all things wait for them. Why, don't you remember that on the very day Mrs. Hopkinson and I and you got the President to sign that patent, that very day one of them d—n fellows turns up from San Francisco or Australia, having taken his own time to get here,—gets here about half an hour after the President had signed the patent and sent it over to the office, finds the right man to introduce him to the President, has a talk with him, makes him sign an order countermanding its issuance, and undoes all that has been done in six years in one hour."

"Yes, but Congress is a tribunal that does not revoke its decrees," said Gashwiler with a return of his old manner; "at least," he added, observing an incredulous shrug in the shoulder of his companion, "at least DURING THE SESSION."

"We shall see," said Wiles, quietly taking his hat.

"We shall see, sir," said the member from Remus with dignity.

CHAPTER XIV

WHAT CULTURE DID FOR IT

There was at this time in the Senate of the United States an eminent and respected gentleman, scholarly, orderly, honorable, and radical,—the fit representative of a scholarly, orderly, honorable, and radical Commonwealth. For many years he had held his trust with conscious rectitude, and a slight depreciation of other forms of merit; and for as many years had been as regularly returned to his seat by his constituency with equally conscious rectitude in themselves and an equal skepticism regarding others. Removed by his nature beyond the reach of certain temptations, and by circumstances beyond even the knowledge of others, his social and political integrity was spotless. An orator and practical debater, his refined tastes kept him from personality, and the public recognition of the complete unselfishness of his motives and the magnitude of his dogmas protected him from scurrility. His principles had never been appealed to by a bribe; he had rarely been approached by an emotion.

A man of polished taste in art and literature, and possessing the means to gratify it, his luxurious home was filled with treasures he had himself collected, and further enhanced by the stamp of his appreciation. His library had not only the elegance of adornment that his wealth could bring and his taste approve, but a certain refined negligence of habitual use, and the easy disorder of the artist's workshop. All this was quickly noted by a young girl who stood on its threshold at the close of a dull January day.

The card that had been brought to the Senator bore the name of "Carmen de Haro"; and modestly in the right hand corner, in almost microscopic script, the further description of herself as "Artist." Perhaps the picturesqueness of the name, and its historic suggestion caught the scholar's taste, for when to his request, through his servant, that she would be kind enough to state her business, she replied as frankly that her business was personal to himself, he directed that she should be admitted. Then entrenching himself behind his library table, overlooking a bastion of books, and a glacis of pamphlets and papers, and throwing into his forehead and eyes an expression of utter disqualification for anything but the business before him, he calmly awaited the intruder.

She came, and for an instant stood, hesitatingly, framing herself as a picture in the door. Mrs. Hopkinson was right,— she had "no style," unless an original and half-foreign quaintness could be called so. There was a desperate attempt visible to combine an American shawl with the habits of a mantilla, and it was always slipping from one shoulder, that was so supple and vivacious as to betray the deficiencies of an education in stays. There was a cluster of black curls around her low forehead, fitting her so closely as to seem to be a part of the seal-skin cap she wore.

Once, from the force of habit, she attempted to put her shawl over her head and talk through the folds gathered under her chin, but an astonished look from the Senator checked her. Nevertheless, he felt relieved, and rising, motioned her to a chair with a heartiness he would have scarcely shown to a

Parisian toilleta. And when, with two or three quick, long steps, she reached his side, and showed, a frank, innocent, but strong and determined little face, feminine only in its flash of eye and beauty of lip and chin curves, he put down the pamphlet he had taken up somewhat ostentatiously, and gently begged to know her business.

I think I have once before spoken of her voice,—an organ more often cultivated by my fair country-women for singing than for speaking, which, considering that much of our practical relations with the sex are carried on without the aid of an opera score, seems a mistaken notion of theirs,—and of its sweetness, gentle inflexion, and musical emphasis. She had the advantage of having been trained in a musical language, and came of a race with whom catarrhs and sore throats were rare. So that in a few brief phrases she sang the Senator into acquiescence as she imparted the plain libretto of her business,—namely, a "desire to see some of his rare engravings."

Now the engravings in question were certain etchings of the early Great Apprentices of the art, and were, I am happy to believe, extremely rare. From my unprofessional view they were exceedingly bad,—showing the mere genesis of something since perfected, but dear, of course, to the true collector's soul. I don't believe that Carmen really admired them either. But the minx knew that the Senator prided himself on having the only "pot-hooks" of the great "A," or the first artistic efforts of "B,"—I leave the real names to be filled in by the connoisseur,—and the Senator became interested. For the last year, two or three of these abominations had been hanging in his study, utterly ignored by the casual visitor. But here was appreciation! "She was," she added, "only a poor young artist, unable to purchase such treasures, but equally unable to resist the opportunity afforded her, even at the risk of seeming bold, or of obtruding upon a great man's privacy," &c. &c.

This flattery, which, if offered in the usual legal tender of the country, would have been looked upon as counterfeit, delivered here in a foreign accent, with a slightly tropical warmth, was accepted by the Senator as genuine. These children of the Sun are so impulsive! We, of course, feel a little pity for the person who thus transcends our standard of good taste and violates our conventional canon,—but they are always sincere. The cold New Englander saw nothing wrong in one or two direct and extravagant compliments, that would have insured his visitor's early dismissal if tendered in the clipped metallic phrases of the Commonwealth he represented.

So that in a few moments the black, curly head of the little artist and the white, flowing locks of the Senator were close together bending over the rack that contained the engravings. It was then that Carmen, listening to a graphic description of the early rise of Art in the Netherlands, forgot herself and put her shawl around her head, holding its folds in her little brown hand. In this situation they were, at different times during the next two hours, interrupted by five Congressmen, three Senators, a Cabinet officer, and a Judge of the Supreme Bench,—each of whom was quickly but courteously dismissed. Popular sentiment, however, broke out in the hall.

"Well, I'm blanked, but this gets me." (The speaker was a Territorial delegate.)

"At his time o' life, too, lookin' over pictures with a gal young enough to be his grandchild." (This from a venerable official, since suspected of various erotic irregularities.)

"She don't handsome any." (The honorable member from Dakota.)

"This accounts for his protracted silence during the sessions." (A serious colleague from the Senator's own State.)

"Oh, blank it all!" (Omnes.)

Four went home to tell their wives. There are few things more touching in the matrimonial compact than the superb frankness with which each confides to each the various irregularities of their friends. It is upon these sacred confidences that the firm foundations of marriage rest unshaken.

Of course the objects of this comment, at least ONE of them, were quite oblivious. "I trust," said Carmen, timidly, when they had for the fourth time regarded in rapt admiration an abominable something by some Dutch wood-chopper, "I trust I am not keeping you from your great friends:"—her pretty eyelids were cast down in tremulous distress:—"I should never forgive myself. Perhaps it is important business of the State?"

"Oh, dear, no! THEY will come again,—it's THEIR business."

The Senator meant it kindly. It was as near the perilous edge of a compliment as your average cultivated Boston man ever ventures, and Carmen picked it up, femininely, by its sentimental end. "And I suppose I shall not trouble you again?"

"I shall always be proud to place the portfolio at your disposal. Command me at any time," said the Senator, with dignity.

"You are kind. You are good," said Carmen, "and I—I'm but,—look you,—only a poor girl from California, that you know not."

"Pardon me, I know your country well." And indeed he could have told her the exact number of bushels of wheat to the acre in her own county of Monterey, its voting population, its political bias. Yet of the more important product before him, after the manner of book-read men, he knew nothing.

Carmen was astonished, but respectful. It transpired presently that she was not aware of the rapid growth of the silk worm in her own district, knew nothing of the Chinese question, and very little of the American mining laws. Upon these questions the Senator enlightened her fully. "Your name is historic, by the way," he said pleasantly. "There was a Knight of Alcantara, a 'De Haro,' one of the emigrants with Las Casas."

Carmen nodded her head quickly, "Yes; my great-great-great-g-r-e-a-t grandfather!"

The Senator stared.

"Oh, yes. I am the niece of Victor Castro, who married my father's sister."

"The Victor Castro of the 'Blue Mass' mine?" asked the Senator abruptly.

"Yes," she said quietly.

Had the Senator been of the Gashwiler type, he would have expressed himself, after the average masculine fashion, by a long-drawn whistle. But his only perceptible appreciation of a sudden astonishment and suspicion in his mind was a lowering of the social thermometer of the room so decided that poor Carmen looked up innocently, chilled, and drew her shawl closer around her shoulders.

"I have something more to ask," said Carmen, hanging her head,—"it is a great, oh, a very great favor."

The Senator had retreated behind his bastion of books again, and was visibly preparing for an assault. He saw it all now. He had been, in some vague way, deluded. He had given confidential audience to the niece of one of the Great Claimants before Congress. The inevitable axe had come to the grindstone. What might not this woman dare ask of him? He was the more implacable that he felt he had already been prepossessed—and honestly prepossessed—in her favor. He was angry with her for having pleased him. Under the icy polish of his manner there were certain Puritan callosities caused by early straight-lacing. He was not yet quite free from his ancestor's cheerful ethics that Nature, as represented by an Impulse, was as much to be restrained as Order represented by a Quaker.

Without apparently noticing his manner, Carmen went on, with a certain potential freedom of style, gesture, and manner scarcely to be indicated in her mere words. "You know, then, I am of Spanish blood, and that, what was my adopted country, our motto was, 'God and Liberty.' It was of you, sir,—the great Emancipator,—the apostle of that Liberty,— the friend of the down-trodden and oppressed,—that I, as a child, first knew. In the histories of this great country I have read of you, I have learned your orations. I have longed to hear you in your own pulpit deliver the creed of my ancestors. To hear you, of yourself, speak, ah! Madre de Dios! what shall I say,—speak the oration eloquent,—to make the—what you call—the debate, that is what I have for so long hoped. Eh! Pardon,—you are thinking me foolish,— wild, eh?—a small child,—eh?"

Becoming more and more dialectical as she went on, she said suddenly, "I have you of myself offended. You are mad of me as a bold, bad child? It is so?"

The Senator, as visibly becoming limp and weak again behind his entrenchments, managed to say, "Oh, no!" then, "really!" and finally, "Tha-a-nks!"

"I am here but for a day. I return to California in a day, as it were to-morrow. I shall never, never hear you speak in your place in the Capitol of this great country?"

The Senator said hastily that he feared—he in fact was convinced—that his duty during this session was required more at his desk, in the committee work, than in speaking, &c., &c.

"Ah," said Carmen sadly, "it is true, then, all this that I have heard. It is true that what they have told me,—that you have given up the great party,—that your voice is not longer heard in the old—what you call this—eh—the old ISSUES?"

"If any one has told you that, Miss De Haro," responded the Senator sharply, "he has spoken foolishly. You have been misinformed. May I ask who—"

"Ah!" said Carmen, "I know not! It is in the air! I am a stranger. Perhaps I am deceived. But it is of all. I say to them, When shall I hear him speak? I go day after day to the Capitol, I watch him,—the great Emancipator,—but it is of business, eh?—it is the claim of that one, it is the tax, eh? it is the impost, it is the post-office, but it is the great speech of human rights—never, NEVER. I say, 'How arrives all this?' And some say, and shake their heads, 'never again he speaks.' He is what you call 'played—yes, it is so, eh?— played out.' I know it not,—it is a word from Bos-ton, perhaps? They say he has—eh, I speak not the English well —the party he has shaken, 'shook,'—yes,—he has the party 'shaken,' eh? It is right,—it is the language of Bos-ton, eh?"

"Permit me to say, Miss De Haro," returned the Senator, rising with some asperity, "that you seem to have been unfortunate in your selection of acquaintances, and still more so in your ideas of the derivations of the English tongue. The—er—the—er—expressions you have quoted are not common to Boston, but emanate, I believe, from the West."

Carmen de Haro contritely buried everything but her black eyes in her shawl.

"No one," he continued, more gently, sitting down again, "has the right to forecast from my past what I intend to do in the future, or designate the means I may choose to serve the principles I hold or the party I represent. Those are MY functions. At the same time, should occasion—or opportunity—for we are within a day or two of the close of the Session—"

"Yes," interrupted Carmen, sadly, "I see,—it will be some business, some claim, something for somebody,—ah! Madre de Dios,—you will not speak, and I—"

"When do you think of returning?" asked the Senator, with grave politeness; "when are we to lose you?"

"I shall stay to the last,—to the end of the Session," said Carmen. "And NOW I shall go." She got up and pulled her shawl viciously over her shoulders, with a pretty pettishness, perhaps the most feminine thing she had done that evening. Possibly, the most genuine.

The Senator smiled affably: "You do not deserve to be disappointed in either case; but it is later than you imagine; let me help you on the shorter distance in my carriage; it is at the door."

He accompanied her gravely to the carriage. As it rolled away, she buried her little figure in its ample cushions and chuckled to herself, albeit a little hysterically. When she had reached her destination, she found herself crying, and hastily, and somewhat angrily, dried her eyes as she drew up at the door of her lodgings.

"How have you prospered?" asked Mr. Harlowe, of counsel for Royal Thatcher, as he gallantly assisted her from the carriage. "I have been waiting here for two hours; your inter-view must have been prolonged,—that was a good sign."

"Don't ask me now," said Carmen, a little savagely, "I'm worn out and tired."

Mr. Harlowe bowed. "I trust you will be better to-morrow, for we expect our friend, Mr. Thatcher."

Carmen's brown cheek flushed slightly. "He should have been here before. Where is he? What was he doing?"

"He was snowed up on the plains. He is coming as fast as steam can carry him; but he may be too late."

Carmen did not reply.

The lawyer lingered. "How did you find the great New-England Senator?" he asked with a slight professional levity.

Carmen was tired, Carmen was worried, Carmen was a little self-reproachful, and she kindled easily. Consequently she said icily:

"I found him A GENTLEMAN!"

CHAPTER XV

HOW IT BECAME UNFINISHED BUSINESS

The closing of the—Congress was not unlike the closing of the several preceding Congresses. There was the same unbusiness-like, impractical haste; the same hurried, unjust, and utterly inadequate adjustment of unfinished, ill-digested business, that would not have been tolerated for a moment by the sovereign people in any private interest they controlled. There were frauds rushed through; there were long-suffering, righteous demands shelved; there were honest, unpaid debts dishonored by scant appropriations; there were closing scenes which only the saving sense of American humor kept from being utterly vile. The actors, the legislators themselves, knew it, and laughed at it; the commentators, the Press, knew it and laughed at it; the audience, the great American people, knew it and laughed at it. And nobody for an instant conceived that it ever, under any circumstances, might be otherwise.

The claim of Roscommon was among the Unfinished Business. The claimant himself, haggard, pathetic, importunate, and obstinate, was among the Unfinished Business. Various Congressmen, more or less interested in the success of the claim, were among the Unfinished Business. The member from Fresno, who had changed his derringer for a speech

Bret Harte

against the claimant, was among the Unfinished Business. The gifted Gashwiler, uneasy in his soul over certain other Unfinished Business in the shape of his missing letters, but dropping oil and honey as he mingled with his brothers, was King of Misrule and Lord of the Unfinished Business. Pretty Mrs. Hopkinson, prudently escorted by her husband, but imprudently ogled by admiring Congressmen, lent the charm of her presence to the finishing of Unfinished Business. One or two editors, who had dreams of a finished financial business, arising out of Unfinished Business, were there also, like ancient bards, to record with paean or threnody the completion of Unfinished Business. Various unclean birds, scenting carrion in Unfinished Business, hovered in the halls or roosted in the Lobby.

The lower house, under the tutelage of the gifted Gashwiler, drank deeply of Roscommon and his intoxicating claim, and passed the half-empty bottle to the Senate as Unfinished Business. But, alas! in the very rush, and storm, and tempest of the unfinishing business, an unlooked-for interruption arose in the person of a great Senator whose power none could oppose, whose right to free and extended utterance at all times none could gainsay. A claim for poultry, violently seized by the army of Sherman during his march through Georgia, from the hen-coop of an alleged loyal Irishman, opened a constitutional question, and with it the lips of the great Senator.

For seven hours he spoke eloquently, earnestly, convincingly. For seven hours the old issues of party and policy were severally taken up and dismissed in the old forcible rhetoric that had early made him famous. Interruptions from other Senators, now forgetful of Unfinished Business, and wild with reanimated party zeal; interruptions from certain Senators mindful of Unfinished Business, and unable to pass the Roscommon bottle, only spurred him to fresh exertion.

The tocsin sounded in the Senate was heard in the lower house. Highly-excited members congregated at the doors of the Senate, and left Unfinished Business to take care of itself.

Left to itself for seven hours, Unfinished Business gnashed its false teeth and tore its wig in impotent fury in corridor and hall. For seven hours the gifted Gashwiler had continued the manufacture of oil and honey, whose sweetness, however, was slowly palling upon the congressional lip; for seven hours Roscommon and friends beat with impatient feet the lobby, and shook fists, more or less discolored, at the distinguished Senator. For seven hours the one or two editors were obliged to sit and calmly compliment the great speech which that night flashed over the wires of a continent with the old electric thrill. And, worse than all, they were obliged to record with it the closing of the—Congress, with more than the usual amount of Unfinished Business.

A little group of friends surrounded the great Senator with hymns of praise and congratulations. Old adversaries saluted him courteously as they passed by with the respect of strong men. A little woman with a shawl drawn over her shoulders, and held with one small brown hand, approached him timidly:

"I speak not the English well," she said gently, "but I have read much. I have read in the plays of your Shakspeare. I would like to say to you the words of Rosalind to Orlando when he did fight: 'Sir you have wrestled well, and have overthrown more than your enemies.'" And with these words she was gone.

Yet not so quickly but that pretty Mrs. Hopkinson, coming, —as Victrix always comes to Victor, to thank the great Senator, albeit the faces of her escorts were shrouded in gloom,—saw the shawled figure disappear.

"There," she said, pinching Wiles mischievously, "there! that's the woman you were afraid of. Look at her. Look at that dress. Ah, Heavens! look at that shawl. Didn't I tell you she had no style?"

"Who is she?" said Wiles sullenly.

"Carmen de Haro, of course," said the lady vivaciously. "What are you hurrying away so for? You're absolutely pulling me along."

Mr. Wiles had just caught sight of the travel-worn face of Royal Thatcher among the crowd that thronged the staircase. Thatcher appeared pale and distrait: Mr. Harlowe, his counsel, at his side, rallied him.

"No one would think you had just got a new lease of your property, and escaped a great swindle. What's the matter with you? Miss De Haro passed us just now. It was she who spoke to the Senator. Why did you not recognize her?"

"I was thinking," said Thatcher gloomily.

"Well, you take things coolly! And certainly you are not very demonstrative towards the woman who saved you to-day. For, as sure as you live, it was she who drew that speech out of the Senator."

Thatcher did not reply, but moved away. He HAD noticed Carmen de Haro, and was about to greet her with mingled pleasure and embarrassment. But he had heard her compliment to the Senator, and this strong, preoccupied, automatic man, who only ten days before had no thought beyond his property, was now thinking more of that compliment to another than of his success; and was beginning to hate the Senator who had saved him, the lawyer who stood beside him, and even the little figure that had tripped down the steps unconscious of him.

CHAPTER XVI

AND WHO FORGOT IT

It was somewhat inconsistent with Royal Thatcher's embarrassment and sensitiveness that he should, on leaving the Capitol, order a carriage and drive directly to the lodgings of Miss De Haro. That on finding she was not at home, he should become again sulky and suspicious, and even be ashamed of the honest impulse that led him there, was, I suppose, manlike and natural. He felt that he had done all the courtesy required; he had promptly answered her dispatch with his presence. If she chose to be absent at such a moment, HE had at least done HIS duty. In short, there was scarcely any absurdity of the imagination which this once practical man did not permit himself to indulge in, yet always with a certain consciousness that he was allowing his feelings to run away with him,—a fact that did not tend to make him better humored, and rather inclined him to place the responsibility of the elopement on somebody else. If Miss De Haro had been home, &c. &c., and not going into ecstasies over speeches, &c. &c., and had attended to her business, i. e., being exactly what he had supposed her to be,—all this would not have happened.

I am aware that this will not heighten the reader's respect for my hero. But I fancy that the imperceptible progress of a sincere passion in the matured strong man is apt to be marked with even more than the usual haste and absurdity of callous youth.

The fever that runs riot in the veins of the robust is apt to pass your ailing weakling by. Possibly there may be some immunity in inoculation. It is Lothario who is always self-possessed and does and says the right thing, while poor honest Coelebs becomes ridiculous with genuine emotion.

He rejoined his lawyer in no very gracious mood. The chambers occupied by Mr. Harlowe were in the basement of a private dwelling once occupied and made historic by an Honorable Somebody, who, however, was remembered only by the landlord and the last tenant. There were various shelves in the walls divided into compartments, sarcastically known as "pigeon holes," in which the dove of peace had never rested, but which still perpetuated, in their legends, the feuds and animosities of suitors now but common dust together. There was a portrait, apparently of a cherub, which on nearer inspection turned out to be a famous English Lord Chancellor in his flowing wig.

There were books with dreary, unenlivening titles,—egotistic always, as recording Smith's opinions on this, and Jones's commentaries on that. There was a hand bill tacked on the wall, which at first offered hilarious suggestions of a circus or a steamboat excursion, but which turned out only to be a sheriff's sale. There were several oddly-shaped packages in newspaper wrappings, mysterious and awful in dark corners, that might have contained forgotten law papers or the previous week's washing of the eminent counsel. There were one or two newspapers, which at first offered entertaining prospects to the waiting client, but always proved to be a law record or a Supreme Court decision. There was the bust of a late distinguished jurist, which apparently had never been dusted since he himself became dust, and had already grown a perceptibly dusty moustache on his severely-judicial upper lip. It was a cheerless place in the sunshine of day; at night, when it ought, by every suggestion of its dusty past, to have been left to the vengeful ghosts, the greater part of whose hopes and passions were recorded and gathered there; when in the dark the dead hands of forgotten men were stretched from their dusty graves to fumble once more for their old title deeds; at night, when it was lit up by flaring gaslight, the hollow mockery of this dissipation was so apparent that people in the streets, looking through the illuminated windows, felt as if the privacy of a family vault had been intruded upon by body-snatchers.

Royal Thatcher glanced around the room, took in all its dreary suggestions in a half-weary, half-indifferent sort of way, and dropped into the lawyer's own revolving chair as that gentleman entered from the adjacent room.

"Well, you got back soon, I see," said Harlowe briskly.

"Yes," said his client, without looking up, and with this notable distinction between himself and all other previous clients, that he seemed absolutely less interested than the lawyer. "Yes, I'm here; and, upon my soul, I don't exactly know why."

"You told me of certain papers you had discovered," said the lawyer suggestively.

"Oh, yes," returned Thatcher with a slight yawn. "I've got here some papers somewhere;"—he began to feel in his coat pocket languidly;—"but, by the way, this is a rather dreary and God-forsaken sort of place! Let's go up to Welker's, and you can look at them over a bottle of champagne."

"After I've looked at them, I've something to show you, myself," said Harlowe; "and as for the champagne, we'll have that in the other room, by and by. At present I want to have my head clear, and yours too,—if you'll oblige me by becoming sufficiently interested in your own affairs to talk to me about them."

Thatcher was gazing abstractedly at the fire. He started. "I dare say," he began, "I'm not very interesting; yet it's possible that my affairs have taken up a little too much of my time. However,—" he stopped, took from his pocket an envelope, and threw it on the desk,—"there are some papers. I don't know what value they may be; that is for you to determine. I don't know that I've any legal right to their possession,—that is for you to say, too. They came to me in a queer way. On the overland journey here I lost my bag, containing my few traps and some letters and papers 'of no value,' as the advertisements say, 'to any but the owner.' Well, the bag was lost, but the stage driver declares that it was stolen by a fellow-passenger,—a man by the name of Giles, or Stiles, or Piles—"

"Wiles," said Harlowe earnestly.

"Yes," continued Thatcher, suppressing a yawn; "yes, I guess you're right,—Wiles. Well, the stage driver, finally believing this, goes to work and quietly and unostentatiously steals—I say, have you got a cigar?"

"I'll get you one."

Harlowe disappeared in the adjoining room. Thatcher dragged Harlowe's heavy, revolving desk chair, which never before had been removed from its sacred position, to the fire, and began to poke the coals abstractedly.

Harlowe reappeared with cigars and matches. Thatcher lit one mechanically, and said, between the pulls:

"Do you—ever—talk—to yourself?"

"No!—why?"

"I thought I heard your voice just now in the other room. Anyhow, this is an awful spooky place. If I stayed here alone half an hour, I'd fancy that the Lord Chancellor up there would step down in his robes, out of his frame, to keep me company."

"Nonsense! When I'm busy, I often sit here and write until after midnight. It's so quiet!"

"D—mnably so!"

"Well, to go back to the papers. Somebody stole your bag, or you lost it. YOU stole—"

"The driver stole," suggested Thatcher, so languidly that it could hardly be called an interruption.

"Well, we'll say the driver stole, and passed over to you as his accomplice, confederate, or receiver, certain papers belonging—"

"See here, Harlowe, I don't feel like joking in a ghostly law office after midnight. Here are your facts. Yuba Bill, the driver, stole a bag from this passenger, Wiles, or Smiles, and handed it to me to insure the return of my own. I found in it some papers concerning my case. There they are. Do with them what you like."

Thatcher turned his eyes again abstractedly to the fire.

Harlowe took out the first paper:

"A-w, this seems to be a telegram. Yes, eh? 'Come to Washington at once.—Carmen de Haro.'"

Thatcher started, blushed like a girl, and hurriedly reached for the paper.

"Nonsense. That's a mistake. A dispatch I mislaid in the envelope."

"I see," said the lawyer dryly.

"I thought I had torn it up," continued Thatcher, after an awkward pause. I regret to say that here that usually truthful man elaborated a fiction. He had consulted it a dozen times a day on the journey, and it was quite worn in its enfoldings. Harlowe's quick eye had noticed this, but he speedily became interested and absorbed in the other papers. Thatcher lapsed into contemplation of the fire.

"Well," said Harlowe, finally turning to his client, "here's enough to unseat Gashwiler, or close his mouth. As to the rest, it's good reading—but I needn't tell you—no LEGAL evidence. But it's proof enough to stop them from ever trying it again,—when the existence of this record is made known. Bribery is a hard thing to fix on a man; the only witness is naturally particeps criminis;—but it would not be easy for them to explain away this rascal's record. One or two things I don't understand: What's this opposite the Hon. X's name, 'Took the medicine nicely, and feels better?' and here, just in the margin, after Y's, 'Must be labored with?'"

"I suppose our California slang borrows largely from the medical and spiritual profession," returned Thatcher. "But isn't it odd that a man should keep a conscientious record of his own villainy?"

Harlowe, a little abashed at his want of knowledge of American metaphor, now felt himself at home. "Well, no. It's not unusual. In one of those books yonder there is the record of a case where a man, who had committed a series of nameless atrocities, extending over a period of years, absolutely kept a memorandum of them in his pocket diary. It was produced in Court. Why, my dear fellow, one half our business arises from the fact that men and women are in the habit of keeping letters and documents that they might—I don't say, you know, that they OUGHT, that's a question of sentiment or ethics—but that they MIGHT destroy."

Thatcher half-mechanically took the telegram of poor Carmen and threw it in the fire. Harlowe noticed the act and smiled.

"I'll venture to say, however, that there's nothing in the bag that YOU lost that need give you a moment's uneasiness. It's only your rascal or fool who carries with him that which makes him his own detective."

"I had a friend," continued Harlowe, "a clever fellow enough, but who was so foolish as to seriously complicate himself with a woman. He was himself the soul of honor, and at the beginning of their correspondence he proposed that they should each return the other's letters with their answer. They did so for years, but it cost him ten thousand dollars and no end of trouble after all."

"Why?" asked Thatcher simply.

"Because he was such an egotistical ass as TO KEEP THE LETTER PROPOSING IT, which she had duly returned, among his papers as a sentimental record. Of course somebody eventually found it."

"Good night," said Thatcher, rising abruptly. "If I stayed here much longer I should begin to disbelieve my own mother."

"I have known of such hereditary traits," returned Harlowe with a laugh. "But come, you must not go without the champagne." He led the way to the adjacent room, which proved to be only the ante-chamber of another, on the threshold of which Thatcher stopped with genuine surprise. It was an elegantly furnished library.

"Sybarite! Why was I never here before?"

"Because you came as a client; to-night you are my guest. All who enter here leave their business, with their hats, in the hall. Look; there isn't a law book on those shelves; that table never was defaced by a title deed or parchment. You look puzzled? Well, it was a whim of mine to put my residence and my work-shop under the same roof, yet so distinct that they would never interfere with each other. You know the house above is let out to lodgers. I occupy the first floor with my mother and sister, and this is my parlor. I do my work in that severe room that fronts the street: here is where I play. A man must have something else in life than mere business. I find it less harmful and expensive to have my pleasure here."

Thatcher had sunk moodily in the embracing arms of an easy chair. He was thinking deeply; he was fond of books too, and, like all men who have fared hard and led wandering lives, he knew the value of cultivated repose. Like all men who have been obliged to sleep under blankets and in the open air, he appreciated the luxuries of linen sheets and a frescoed roof. It is, by the way, only your sick city clerk or your dyspeptic clergyman who fancy that they have found in the bad bread, fried steaks, and frowzy flannels of mountain picknicking the true art of living. And it is a somewhat notable fact that your true mountaineer or your gentleman who has been obliged to honestly "rough it," does not, as a general thing, write books about its advantages, or implore their fellow mortals to come and share their solitude and their discomforts.

Thoroughly appreciating the taste and comfort of Harlowe's library, yet half-envious of its owner, and half-suspicious that his own earnest life for the past few years might have been different, Thatcher suddenly started from his seat and walked towards a parlor easel, whereon stood a picture. It was Carmen de Haro's first sketch of the furnace and the mine.

"I see you are taken with that picture," said Harlowe, pausing with the champagne bottle in his hand. "You show your good taste. It's been much admired. Observe how splendidly that firelight plays over the sleeping face of that figure, yet brings out by very contrast its almost death-like repose. Those rocks are powerfully handled; what a suggestion of mystery in those shadows! You know the painter?"

Thatcher murmured, "Miss De Haro," with a new and rather odd self-consciousness in speaking her name.

"Yes. And you know the story of the picture of course?"

Thatcher thought he didn't. Well, no; in fact, he did not remember.

"Why, this recumbent figure was an old Spanish lover of hers, whom she believed to have been murdered there. It's a ghastly fancy, isn't it?"

Two things annoyed Thatcher: first the epithet "lover," as

applied to Concho by another man; second, that the picture belonged to him: and what the d—l did she mean by—

"Yes," he broke out finally, "but how did YOU get it?"

"Oh, I bought it of her. I've been a sort of patron of her ever since I found out how she stood towards us. As she was quite alone here in Washington, my mother and sister have taken her up, and have been doing the social thing."

"How long since?" asked Thatcher.

"Oh, not long. The day she telegraphed you, she came here to know what she could do for us, and when I said nothing could be done except to keep Congress off, why, she went and DID IT. For SHE, and she alone, got that speech out of the Senator. But," he added, a little mischievously, "you seem to know very little about her?"

"No!—I—that is—I've been very busy lately," returned Thatcher, staring at the picture. "Does she come here often?"

"Yes, lately, quite often; she was here this evening with mother; was here, I think, when you came."

Thatcher looked intently at Harlowe. But that gentleman's face betrayed no confusion. Thatcher refilled his glass a little awkwardly, tossed off the liquor at a draught, and rose to his feet.

"Come, old fellow, you're not going now. I shan't permit it," said Harlowe, laying his hand kindly on his client's shoulder. "You're out of sorts! Stay here with me to-night. Our accommodations are not large, but are elastic. I can bestow you comfortably until morning. Wait here a moment while I give the necessary orders."

Thatcher was not sorry to be left alone. In the last half hour he had become convinced that his love for Carmen de Haro had been in some way most dreadfully abused. While HE was hard at work in California, she was being introduced in Washington society by parties with eligible brothers who bought her paintings. It is a relief to the truly jealous mind to indulge in plurals. Thatcher liked to think that she was already beset by hundreds of brothers.

He still kept staring at the picture. By and by it faded away in part, and a very vivid recollection of the misty, midnight, moonlit walk he had once taken with her came back, and refilled the canvas with its magic. He saw the ruined furnace; the dark, overhanging masses of rock, the trembling intricacies of foliage, and, above all, the flash of dark eyes under a mantilla at his shoulder. What a fool he had been! Had he not really been as senseless and stupid as this very Concho, lying here like a log? And she had loved that man. What a fool she must have thought him that evening! What a snob she must think him now!

He was startled by a slight rustling in the passage, that ceased almost as he turned. Thatcher looked towards the door of the outer office, as if half expecting that the Lord Chancellor, like the commander in Don Juan, might have accepted his thoughtless invitation. He listened again; everything was still. He was conscious of feeling ill at ease and a trifle nervous. What a long time Harlowe took to make his preparations. He would look out in the hall. To do this it was necessary to turn up the gas. He did so, and in his confusion turned it out!

Where were the matches? He remembered that there was a bronze something on the table that, in the irony of modern decorative taste, might hold ashes or matches, or anything of an unpicturesque character. He knocked something over, evidently the ink,—something else,—this time a champagne glass. Becoming reckless, and now groping at random in the ruins, he overturned the bronze Mercury on the center table, and then sat down hopelessly in his chair. And then a pair of velvet fingers slid into his, with the matches, and this audible, musical statement:

"It is a match you are seeking? Here is of them."

Thatcher flushed, embarrassed, nervous,—feeling the ridiculousness of saying, "Thank you" to a dark somebody, —struck the match, beheld by its brief, uncertain glimmer Carmen de Haro beside him, burned his fingers, coughed, dropped the match, and was cast again into outer darkness.

"Let me try!"

Carmen struck a match, jumped briskly on the chair, lit the gas, jumped lightly down again, and said: "You do like to sit in the dark,—eh? So am I—sometimes—alone."

"Miss De Haro," said Thatcher, with sudden, honest earnestness, advancing with outstretched hands, "believe me I am sincerely delighted, overjoyed, again to meet—"

She had, however, quickly retreated as he approached, ensconcing herself behind the high back of a large antique chair, on the cushion of which she knelt. I regret to add also that she slapped his outstretched fingers a little sharply with her inevitable black fan as he still advanced.

"We are not in California. It is Washington. It is after midnight. I am a poor girl, and I have to lose—what you call—'a character.' You shall sit over there,"—she pointed to the sofa,—"and I shall sit here;" she rested her boyish head on the top of the chair; "and we shall talk, for I have to speak to you, Don Royal."

Thatcher took the seat indicated, contritely, humbly, submissively. Carmen's little heart was touched. But she still went on over the back of the chair.

"Don Royal," she said, emphasizing each word at him with her fan, "before I saw you,—ever knew of you,—I was a child. Yes, I was but a child! I was a bold, bad child;—and I was what you call a—a—'forgaire'!"

"A what?" asked Thatcher, hesitating between a smile and a sigh.

"A forgaire!" continued Carmen demurely. "I did of myself write the names of ozzer peoples;" when Carmen was excited she lost the control of the English tongue; "I did write just to please myself;—it was my onkle that did make of it money;—you understand, eh? Shall you not speak? Must I again hit you?"

"Go on," said Thatcher laughing.

"I did find out, when I came to you at the mine, that I had forged against you the name of Micheltorena. I to the lawyer went, and found that it was so—of a verity—so! so! all the time. Look at me not now, Don Royal;—it is a 'forgaire' you stare at."

"Carmen!"

"Hoosh! Shall I have to hit you again? I did overlook all the papers. I found the application: it was written by me. There."

She tossed over the back of her chair an envelope to Thatcher. He opened it.

"I see," he said gently, "you repossessed yourself of it!"

"What is that—'r-r-r-e—possess'?"

"Why!"—Thatcher hesitated—"you got possession of this paper,—this innocent forgery,—again."

"Oh! You think me a thief as well as a 'forgaire.' Go away! Get up. Get out."

"My dear girl—"

"Look at the paper! Will you? Oh, you silly!"

Thatcher looked at the paper. In paper, handwriting, age, and stamp it was identical with the formal, clerical application of Garcia for the grant. The indorsement of Micheltorena was unquestionably genuine. BUT THE APPLICATION WAS MADE FOR ROYAL THATCHER. And his own signature was imitated to the life.

"I had but one letter of yours wiz your name," said Carmen apologetically; "and it was the best poor me could do."

"Why, you blessed little goose and angel," said Thatcher, with the bold, mixed metaphor of amatory genius, "don't you see—"

"Ah, you don't like it,—it is not good?"

"My darling!"

"Hoosh! There is also an 'old cat' up stairs. And now I have here a character. WILL you sit down? Is it of a necessity that up and down you should walk and awaken the whole house? There!"—she had given him a vicious dab with her fan as he passed. He sat down.

"And you have not seen me nor written to me for a year?"

"Carmen!"

"Sit down, you bold, bad boy. Don't you see it is of business that you and I talk down here; and it is of business that ozzer people up stairs are thinking. Eh?"

"D—n business! See here, Carmen, my darling, tell me"—I regret to say he had by this time got hold of the back of Carmen's chair—"tell me, my own little girl,—about—about that Senator. You remember what you said to him?"

"Oh, the old man? Oh, THAT was business. And you say of business, 'd—n.'"

"Carmen!"

"Don Royal!"

*****

Although Miss Carmen had recourse to her fan frequently during this interview, the air must have been chilly, for a moment later, on his way down stairs, poor Harlowe, a sufferer from bronchitis, was attacked with a violent fit of coughing, which troubled him all the way down.

"Well," he said, as he entered the room, "I see you have found Mr. Thatcher, and shown those papers. I trust you have, for you've certainly had time enough. I am sent by mother to dismiss you all to bed."

Carmen still in the arm chair, covered with her mantilla, did not speak.

"I suppose you are by this time lawyer enough to know," continued Harlowe, "that Miss De Haro's papers, though ingenious, are not legally available, unless—"

"I chose to make her a witness. Harlowe! you're a good fellow! I don't mind saying to you that these are papers I prefer that my WIFE should not use. We'll leave it for the present—Unfinished Business."

They did. But one evening our hero brought Mrs. Royal Thatcher a paper containing a touching and beautiful tribute to the dead Senator.

"There, Carmen, love, read that. Don't you feel a little ashamed of your—your—your lobbying—"

"No," said Carmen promptly. "It was business,—and if all lobbying business was as honest,—well?—"

ABOUT THE AUTHOR

 **Francis Bret Harte** (August 25, 1836–May 6, 1902) was an American author and poet, best remembered for his accounts of pioneering life in California.

Born in Albany, New York, Harte moved to California in 1853, later working there in a number of capacities, including miner, teacher, messenger, and journalist. He spent part of his life in the northern California coast town now known as Arcata, at the time it was just a mining camp on Humboldt Bay.

His first literary efforts, including poetry and prose, appeared in The Californian, an early literary journal edited by Charles Henry Webb. In 1868 he became editor of The Overland Monthly, another new literary magazine, but this one more in tune with the pioneering spirit of excitement in California. His story, "The Luck of Roaring Camp," appeared in the magazine's second edition, propelling Harte to nationwide fame.

As an established literary figure, he was appointed to the position of United States Consul in the town of Krefeld, Germany in 1878 and Glasgow in 1880. In 1885 he settled in London. During the thirty years he spent in Europe, he never abandoned writing, and maintained a prodigious output of stories that retained the freshness of his earlier work. He died in England in 1902.

Choose from Thousands of 1stWorldLibrary Classics By

A. M. Barnard
Ada Leverson
Adolphus William Ward
Aesop
Agatha Christie
Alexander Aaronsohn
Alexander Kielland
Alexandre Dumas
Alfred Gatty
Alfred Ollivant
Alice Duer Miller
Alice Turner Curtis
Alice Dunbar
Allen Chapman
Alleyne Ireland
Ambrose Bierce
Amelia E. Barr
Amory H. Bradford
Andrew Lang
Andrew McFarland Davis
Andy Adams
Angela Brazil
Anna Alice Chapin
Anna Sewell
Annie Besant
Annie Hamilton Donnell
Annie Payson Call
Annie Roe Carr
Annonaymous
Anton Chekhov
Archibald Lee Fletcher
Arnold Bennett
Arthur C. Benson
Arthur Conan Doyle
Arthur M. Winfield
Arthur Ransome
Arthur Schnitzler
Arthur Train
Atticus
B.H. Baden-Powell
B. M. Bower
B. C. Chatterjee
Baroness Emmuska Orczy
Baroness Orczy
Basil King
Bayard Taylor
Ben Macomber
Bertha Muzzy Bower
Bjornstjerne Bjornson

Booth Tarkington
Boyd Cable
Bram Stoker
C. Collodi
C. E. Orr
C. M. Ingleby
Carolyn Wells
Catherine Parr Traill
Charles A. Eastman
Charles Amory Beach
Charles Dickens
Charles Dudley Warner
Charles Farrar Browne
Charles Ives
Charles Kingsley
Charles Klein
Charles Hanson Towne
Charles Lathrop Pack
Charles Romyn Dake
Charles Whibley
Charles Willing Beale
Charlotte M. Braeme
Charlotte M. Yonge
Charlotte Perkins Stetson
Clair W. Hayes
Clarence Day Jr.
Clarence E. Mulford
Clemence Housman
Confucius
Coningsby Dawson
Cornelis DeWitt Wilcox
Cyril Burleigh
D. H. Lawrence
Daniel Defoe
David Garnett
Dinah Craik
Don Carlos Janes
Donald Keyhoe
Dorothy Kilner
Dougan Clark
Douglas Fairbanks
E. Nesbit
E. P. Roe
E. Phillips Oppenheim
E. S. Brooks
Earl Barnes
Edgar Rice Burroughs
Edith Van Dyne
Edith Wharton

Edward Everett Hale
Edward J. O'Biren
Edward S. Ellis
Edwin L. Arnold
Eleanor Atkins
Eleanor Hallowell Abbott
Eliot Gregory
Elizabeth Gaskell
Elizabeth McCracken
Elizabeth Von Arnim
Ellem Key
Emerson Hough
Emilie F. Carlen
Emily Bronte
Emily Dickinson
Enid Bagnold
Enilor Macartney Lane
Erasmus W. Jones
Ernie Howard Pie
Ethel May Dell
Ethel Turner
Ethel Watts Mumford
Eugene Sue
Eugenie Foa
Eugene Wood
Eustace Hale Ball
Evelyn Everett-green
Everard Cotes
F. H. Cheley
F. J. Cross
F. Marion Crawford
Fannie E. Newberry
Federick Austin Ogg
Ferdinand Ossendowski
Fergus Hume
Florence A. Kilpatrick
Fremont B. Deering
Francis Bacon
Francis Darwin
Frances Hodgson Burnett
Frances Parkinson Keyes
Frank Gee Patchin
Frank Harris
Frank Jewett Mather
Frank L. Packard
Frank V. Webster
Frederic Stewart Isham
Frederick Trevor Hill
Frederick Winslow Taylor

Friedrich Kerst
Friedrich Nietzsche
Fyodor Dostoyevsky
G.A. Henty
G.K. Chesterton
Gabrielle E. Jackson
Garrett P. Serviss
Gaston Leroux
George A. Warren
George Ade
Geroge Bernard Shaw
George Cary Eggleston
George Durston
George Ebers
George Eliot
George Gissing
George MacDonald
George Meredith
George Orwell
George Sylvester Viereck
George Tucker
George W. Cable
George Wharton James
Gertrude Atherton
Gordon Casserly
Grace E. King
Grace Gallatin
Grace Greenwood
Grant Allen
Guillermo A. Sherwell
Gulielma Zollinger
Gustav Flaubert
H. A. Cody
H. B. Irving
H.C. Bailey
H. G. Wells
H. H. Munro
H. Irving Hancock
H. R. Naylor
H. Rider Haggard
H. W. C. Davis
Haldeman Julius
Hall Caine
Hamilton Wright Mabie
Hans Christian Andersen
Harold Avery
Harold McGrath
Harriet Beecher Stowe
Harry Castlemon
Harry Coghill
Harry Houidini

Hayden Carruth
Helent Hunt Jackson
Helen Nicolay
Hendrik Conscience
Hendy David Thoreau
Henri Barbusse
Henrik Ibsen
Henry Adams
Henry Ford
Henry Frost
Henry James
Henry Jones Ford
Henry Seton Merriman
Henry W Longfellow
Herbert A. Giles
Herbert Carter
Herbert N. Casson
Herman Hesse
Hildegard G. Frey
Homer
Honore De Balzac
Horace B. Day
Horace Walpole
Horatio Alger Jr.
Howard Pyle
Howard R. Garis
Hugh Lofting
Hugh Walpole
Humphry Ward
Ian Maclaren
Inez Haynes Gillmore
Irving Bacheller
Isabel Cecilia Williams
Isabel Hornibrook
Israel Abrahams
Ivan Turgenev
J.G.Austin
J. Henri Fabre
J. M. Barrie
J. M. Walsh
J. Macdonald Oxley
J. R. Miller
J. S. Fletcher
J. S. Knowles
J. Storer Clouston
J. W. Duffield
Jack London
Jacob Abbott
James Allen
James Andrews
James Baldwin

James Branch Cabell
James DeMille
James Joyce
James Lane Allen
James Lane Allen
James Oliver Curwood
James Oppenheim
James Otis
James R. Driscoll
Jane Abbott
Jane Austen
Jane L. Stewart
Janet Aldridge
Jens Peter Jacobsen
Jerome K. Jerome
Jessie Graham Flower
John Buchan
John Burroughs
John Cournos
John F. Kennedy
John Gay
John Glasworthy
John Habberton
John Joy Bell
John Kendrick Bangs
John Milton
John Philip Sousa
John Taintor Foote
Jonas Lauritz Idemil Lie
Jonathan Swift
Joseph A. Altsheler
Joseph Carey
Joseph Conrad
Joseph E. Badger Jr
Joseph Hergesheimer
Joseph Jacobs
Jules Vernes
Julian Hawthrone
Julie A Lippmann
Justin Huntly McCarthy
Kakuzo Okakura
Karle Wilson Baker
Kate Chopin
Kenneth Grahame
Kenneth McGaffey
Kate Langley Bosher
Kate Langley Bosher
Katherine Cecil Thurston
Katherine Stokes
L. A. Abbot
L. T. Meade

L. Frank Baum
Latta Griswold
Laura Dent Crane
Laura Lee Hope
Laurence Housman
Lawrence Beasley
Leo Tolstoy
Leonid Andreyev
Lewis Carroll
Lewis Sperry Chafer
Lilian Bell
Lloyd Osbourne
Louis Hughes
Louis Joseph Vance
Louis Tracy
Louisa May Alcott
Lucy Fitch Perkins
Lucy Maud Montgomery
Luther Benson
Lydia Miller Middleton
Lyndon Orr
M. Corvus
M. H. Adams
Margaret E. Sangster
Margret Howth
Margaret Vandercook
Margaret W. Hungerford
Margret Penrose
Maria Edgeworth
Maria Thompson Daviess
Mariano Azuela
Marion Polk Angellotti
Mark Overton
Mark Twain
Mary Austin
Mary Catherine Crowley
Mary Cole
Mary Hastings Bradley
Mary Roberts Rinehart
Mary Rowlandson
M. Wollstonecraft Shelley
Maud Lindsay
Max Beerbohm
Myra Kelly
Nathaniel Hawthrone
Nicolo Machiavelli
O. F. Walton
Oscar Wilde

Owen Johnson
P.G. Wodehouse
Paul and Mabel Thorne
Paul G. Tomlinson
Paul Severing
Percy Brebner
Percy Keese Fitzhugh
Peter B. Kyne
Plato
Quincy Allen
R. Derby Holmes
R. L. Stevenson
R. S. Ball
Rabindranath Tagore
Rahul Alvares
Ralph Bonehill
Ralph Henry Barbour
Ralph Victor
Ralph Waldo Emmerson
Rene Descartes
Ray Cummings
Rex Beach
Rex E. Beach
Richard Harding Davis
Richard Jefferies
Richard Le Gallienne
Robert Barr
Robert Frost
Robert Gordon Anderson
Robert L. Drake
Robert Lansing
Robert Lynd
Robert Michael Ballantyne
Robert W. Chambers
Rosa Nouchette Carey
Rudyard Kipling
Saint Augustine
Samuel B. Allison
Samuel Hopkins Adams
Sarah Bernhardt
Sarah C. Hallowell
Selma Lagerlof
Sherwood Anderson
Sigmund Freud
Standish O'Grady
Stanley Weyman
Stella Benson
Stella M. Francis

Stephen Crane
Stewart Edward White
Stijn Streuvels
Swami Abhedananda
Swami Parmananda
T. S. Ackland
T. S. Arthur
The Princess Der Ling
Thomas A. Janvier
Thomas A Kempis
Thomas Anderton
Thomas Bailey Aldrich
Thomas Bulfinch
Thomas De Quincey
Thomas Dixon
Thomas H. Huxley
Thomas Hardy
Thomas More
Thornton W. Burgess
U. S. Grant
Upton Sinclair
Valentine Williams
Various Authors
Vaughan Kester
Victor Appleton
Victor G. Durham
Victoria Cross
Virginia Woolf
Wadsworth Camp
Walter Camp
Walter Scott
Washington Irving
Wilbur Lawton
Wilkie Collins
Willa Cather
Willard F. Baker
William Dean Howells
William le Queux
W. Makepeace Thackeray
William W. Walter
William Shakespeare
Winston Churchill
Yei Theodora Ozaki
Yogi Ramacharaka
Young E. Allison
Zane Grey

www.ingramcontent.com/pod-product-compliance
Lightning Source LLC
Chambersburg PA
CBHW051835170626
46807CB00003B/1186